PERFECT BLOCKS
in minutes

the *Make It* **Simpler** way

Anita Grossman Solomon

Revolutionary Technique
One-Piece Paper Foundations to Fold & Sew • 60 Traditional Blocks

C&T PUBLISHING

Text and Artwork © 2004 Anita Grossman Solomon

Artwork © 2004 C&T Publishing

Publisher: Amy Marson

Editorial Director: Gailen Runge

Acquisitions Editor: Jan Grigsby

Editors: Jan Grigsby and Liz Aneloski

Technical Editors: Catherine Comyns and Cynthia Keyes Hilton

Copyeditor: Stacy Chamness

Proofreader: Wordfirm

Cover Designer: Kristy Konitzer

Production Artist: Kirstie L. McCormick

Illustrator: John Heisch

Production Assistant: Luke Mulks

Photography: Sharon Risedorph and C&T Publishing unless otherwise noted

Published by C&T Publishing, Inc., P.O. Box 1456, Lafayette, California, 94549

Library of Congress Cataloging-in-Publication Data

ISBN 0-7394-4986-9

Book Club Edition

Printed In U.S.A.

DEDICATION

My late father, Stanley Grossman, was my steadfast supporter. One crisp fall morning, he met me at the Greater Buffalo Airport to take me to my first quilting seminar at the Amherst Museum. As we pulled up to the museum, he looked over at me and smiled, not knowing what to make of the cavalcade of sewing machines at the entrance. I think that he somehow knew that those first explorations would lead to something. I dedicate this book to him.

ACKNOWLEDGMENTS

My husband, Horace, continues to encourage, support, and accommodate my dreams, understanding that both he and the art of quilting are my true passions.

Many kindnesses were extended to me in my first book, *Make It Simpler Paper Piecing*, and it has been a joy to continue this collaboration with so many fine individuals throughout the evolution of this second book. Each of the people listed on pages 93–94 gave me their time, ideas, and support, for which I am unendingly grateful. Susan Stauber is especially appreciated for her devotion to the project.

Liz Aneloski and Jan Grigsby; Dorothea Hahn, Georgette Hasiotis, Oana Ivanov, Claudia Jaffe, Miriam Janove, Suzanne Lemakis, Julia Morelli, Norma Torres

Jamie Arcuri and Donna Wilder, FreeSpirit Fabrics, New York, NY

Genie Becknell, Printed Treasures by Milliken, Spartanburg, SC

Emily Cohen, Timeless Treasures Fabrics, Inc., New York, NY

Janet deCarteret, BlockButler, Inc., Bellevue, WA

Karen Diehl and Dianne Giancola, Prym-Dritz Corp., Spartanburg, SC

Michele Hirschberg, Clairmont-Nichols Opticians, New York, NY

Cathy Izzo and the staff of the City Quilter, New York, NY

Gail Kessler and John Conneely, Andover Fabrics, New York, NY

Mary Gay Leahy, Fairfield Processing Corp., Danbury, CT

Penny McMorris and the Electric Quilt Company, Bowling Green, OH

Kathy Miller and Michael Steiner, Michael Miller Fabrics, New York, NY

Julie Scribner and Irwin Bear, P&B Textiles, Burlingame, CA

Anita Grossman Solomon

INTRODUCTION

Make It Simpler Paper Piecing means that your points and intersections will always automatically match when you sew a block together. The foundation patterns are never cut apart so, unlike Humpty Dumpty, you never have to put a foundation back together again. Perfect blocks will happen automatically before your eyes, in minutes.

I'm reminded of what friends on opposite coasts confided in me. Each had been enlisted to test the Make It Simpler technique and was sworn to secrecy. Each happened to be participating in a paper-pieced block swap. And each told me she abandoned the swap block instructions for the piecing techniques and secrets you will find in this book. Neither of these quilters would go back to conventional paper piecing once she had tried Make It Simpler Paper Piecing.

One pleasure I encountered while writing this quilt book was going to my sewing area to try out an idea, rather than taking care of household chores. Another was cutting into fabric that had been saved for just the right occasion. But the greatest pleasure of all was being able to deconstruct and reconstruct blocks that I could never paper piece to my satisfaction, such as Single Irish Chain (pages 67–69) or Necktie (pages 33–35). Now, blocks full of angles, blocks that are visually complex, are perfectly assembled in minutes using this technique.

The easiest blocks to sew have only one or two pieces in a subunit and few folds. A Plain Block (pages 63–64) is the easiest: glue the nine pieces in place and sew only four

seams. You'll be surprised by the cool way that Aunt Eliza's Star (pages 77–79) is assembled. There isn't a quarter-square triangle used in the block. Really. Since the Necktie block is foundation pieced, there are no set-in seams, even though the center knot is an unpieced square. The Single Irish Chain is my personal engineering triumph.

As in *Make It Simpler Paper Piecing*, the quilt designs, patterns, and templates for this book originated with EQ5, a computer software program from The Electric Quilt Company. The patterns with a "Brackman number" can be found in BlockBase, an electronic version of Barbara Brackman's *Encyclopedia of Pieced Quilt Patterns*. The foundation patterns in this book are my own original designs.

Be sure to read the Techniques section, Ask Anita, and all of the Helpful Hints before you begin sewing to maximize your understanding of the technique. You will be smiling the moment you open your first block and forever after as you find you've amassed a pile of Perfect Blocks.

TABLE OF
CONTENTS

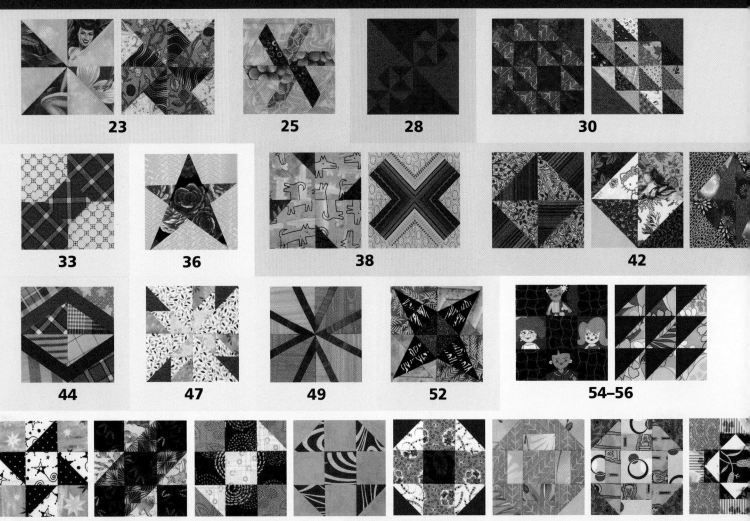

54–56

61 **63** **65**

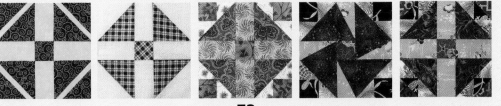

67 **70**

72

77

80 **83**

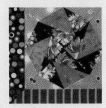

86 **89** **91**

Technique at a Glance

This section is an overview of the Make It Simpler Paper Piecing technique. Complete instructions begin on page 8.

1. Foundation (right side up)

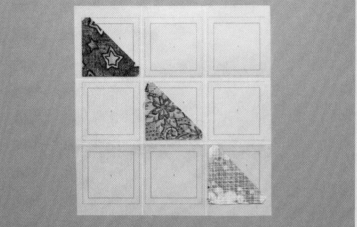

2. Turn the previously-folded paper foundation over (wrong side up). Secure the light triangles to the foundation, place the dark triangles on top of their corresponding light triangles, and secure to the foundation.

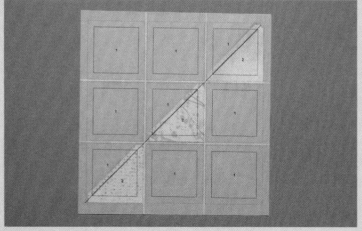

3. Turn the foundation paper over (right side up) and sew on the line.

4. Press the triangles open. Place the fabric squares on the foundation and secure.

5. Fold on one of the seamlines.

6. Sew the seam.

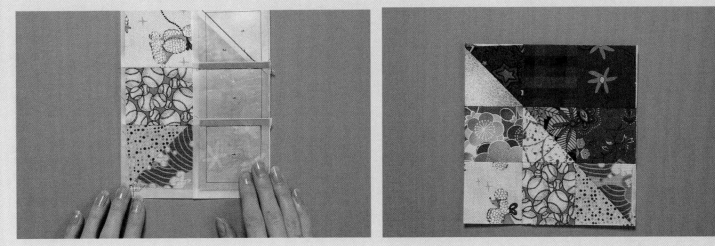

7. Repeat for all seams.

8. The finished block!

The Make It Simpler Techniques For Paper Piecing

Nine-Patch Variation 1706

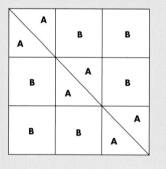

2½" x 2½" □

Nine-Patch Variation

B

Cut 3 light

Cut 3 dark

2⅞" ◺

Nine-Patch Variation

A

Cut 3 light

Cut 3 dark

HELPFUL HINTS

Replacing the two triangles in the center square with a simple 2½" square of red fabric creates the Split Nine-Patch block, native to New Jersey. Like the traditional Log Cabin, the Nine-Patch Variation and the Split Nine-Patch can be arranged in the Barn Raising or Streak of Lightning settings. The Straight Furrows setting is more versatile because it can be made with an odd number of blocks.

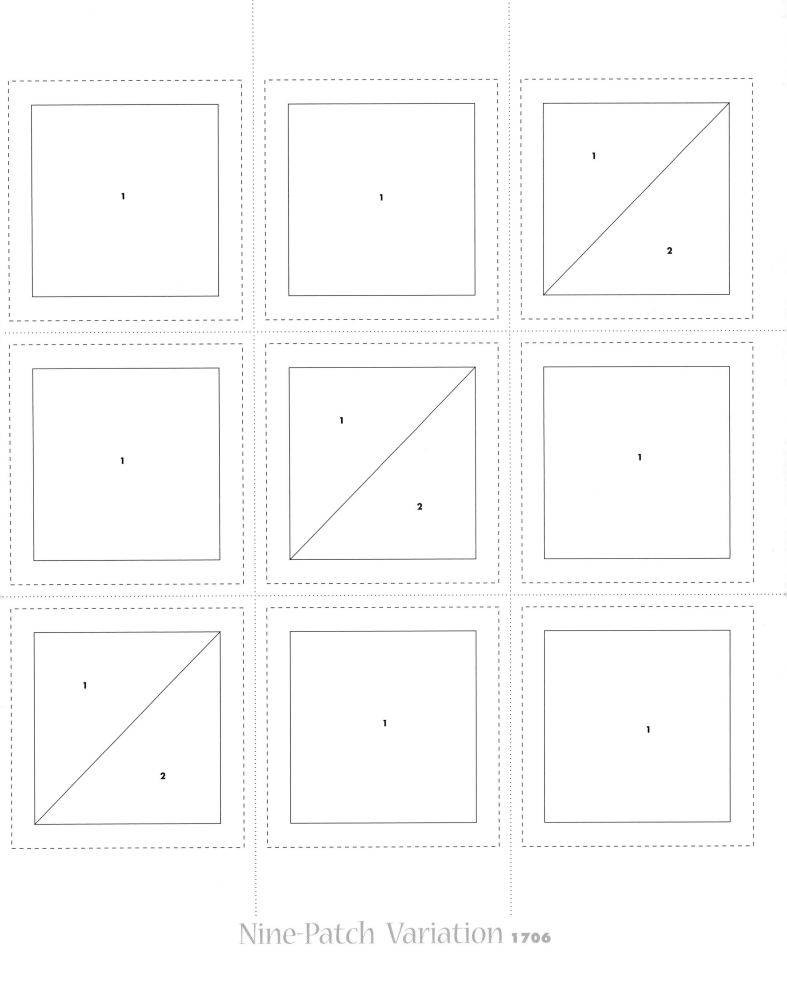

Nine-Patch Variation 1706

Getting Started

The Nine-Patch Variation is a traditional block dating from the nineteenth century. It is simple to make and demonstrates the Make It Simpler Paper Piecing techniques used to construct the other blocks in this book.

Preparation

1. Photocopy a foundation pattern from the book onto translucent paper. To evaluate the accuracy of the copy machine, lay the copy on top of the original. If the lines match up perfectly, make additional photocopies of the pattern onto translucent paper. You will need at least one for the mock-up and one for sewing. Never copy a photocopy of a foundation; always use the original in the book to keep copier distortion to a minimum.

Don't worry if the translucent paper photocopy of a foundation pattern is missing part of the outside dashed line at the edge of the pattern. This will not affect construction of the block. As detailed on page 18, the printed edge of the foundation is never used as a trimming guide.

Photocopy the templates onto ordinary paper.

❀ TIP

May I photocopy the foundation patterns onto white copy paper instead of onto translucent paper? Well, you wouldn't be making it simpler. It is more difficult to crease and fold copy paper and you can't see through it very well. Nothing beats translucent paper for ease. (Simple Foundations paper is available

from C&T Publishing.) I would also avoid combining different brands of foundation paper in one project, because they may not yield identical results. To avoid confusion, prepare, copy, and label separate templates for template pieces that also have a reverse, such as A (regular) and AR (reversed).

❀ TIP

Do I have to worry about "mirror imaging" when I photocopy? No. The foundations in the book are already mirrored for you.

2. Trim away excess foundation paper, leaving about ¾" around the block. This makes sewing at the machine more manageable.

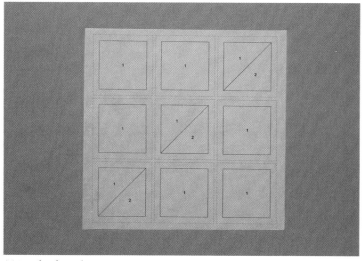

Trim the foundation.

3. Choose and cut the fabrics. For each block, select 6 light and 6 dark fabrics. Cut 3 light and 3 dark 2½" squares. Also cut 3 light and 3 dark 2⅞" squares, then cut these in half diagonally. Use the triangle template to trim off the base points, so they won't extend into the gutters and cover any folds on the foundation paper (Step 5, page 12). You will have 6 triangles left over.

How do you make and use the templates?

Photocopy the templates on regular copy paper and cut them out. If a template gets misplaced, just make another copy of it. First, cut the fabric using the dimensions on the template. Then, place the template flush along the edge of the fabric. Trim off the excess fabric around the template with a rotary cutter, using a ruler to protect your fingers when necessary. You could also hold the template and fabric in one hand while trimming off the excess with a pair of scissors.

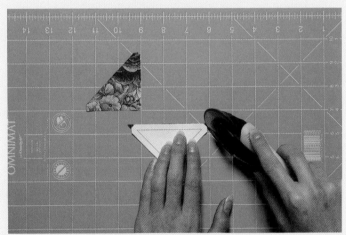

Use a rotary cutter to trim excess fabric.

Cut fabric for only one block right now. This will give you the opportunity to alter your fabric choices or to modify your cutting plan.

Use a 2½" acrylic square to cut many squares at once from scraps. For the triangles, cut (or sometimes tear) a strip from the yardage, approximately ½" wider than necessary, because you don't want to wrestle with a large piece of fabric. If you have half a yard of fabric, tear it along the length so that you have a piece measuring about 18" x 3½". I prefer strips from the length (parallel to the selvage), because I find them more stable to work with. Fold the strip to a length that you can comfortably cut 2⅞" squares from. I usually cut through 5 layers of fabric at once and then cut on the diagonal to yield 10 triangles, then trim the excess fabric.

TIP

Because I can easily gauge the fabric to cut for the template shapes, must I pay attention to the rotary cutting information? Yes, it's a matter of ensuring good grainline placement in the block, especially when it comes to triangles. Depending on their placement in the block, different cuts of triangles are required. Half-square triangles are made from squares cut once on the diagonal to yield a pair of triangles. Each will have only one side on the bias. Quarter-square triangles are made from cutting a square of fabric twice, once on each diagonal. This yields 4 triangles, each with 2 bias sides.

Half-Square Triangle   Quarter-Square Triangle

4. Make a fabric mock-up by placing the cut squares and triangles on the unprinted side of an unfolded foundation. The Nine-Patch Variation visually divides the block into 2 large triangles, one of which reads darker (or lighter) than the other.

❄ TIP

What is a mock-up? A mock-up is a preview of the completed block. The entire block is laid out in position prior to sewing. It's an opportunity to view the relationship of one fabric to another to check color harmonies, interactions between fabrics, and to correct placement.

Mock-up of block

❄ TIP

I have paper pieced before and I know where every fabric will go. I want to skip making a mock-up. Is that okay? No. Sometimes when I skipped the mock-up, I picked up the wrong piece to sew onto the foundation pattern.

5. Fold and crease the foundation. The dotted lines on the pattern indicate the fold lines. First fold the unprinted sides of the foundation together. The seam and fold lines are easier to see this way. Then fold the paper back the other way along the same line, placing printed sides together, and crease sharply. Repeat for all fold lines. The printed lines are more visible on a light table or white surface. I fold my foundation against the TV screen. While the TV is on, static electricity holds the foundation.

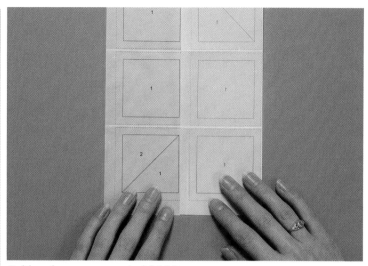

Fold and crease on vertical fold lines.

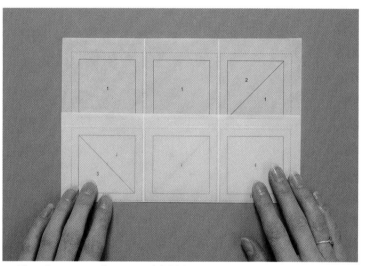

Fold and crease on horizontal fold lines.

Sewing

1. Set up the sewing machine with a #90 needle. Set the stitch length to approximately 15–20 stitches per inch. The stitches should be as small as possible while still fitting the point of a seam ripper. Match the thread to the fabric. For example, when sewing dark fabrics together, use matching dark thread. Suitable threads make seams nearly invisible.

Always place the fabric pieces on the unprinted side of the foundation and sew on the printed side. The printed side of the foundation will be the back of the block when you have finished. You can see through the translucent foundation paper, but the numbers or words will appear backward as you place the fabrics. If you place the pieces on the printed side by mistake, you won't see the sewing lines on the unprinted side of the pattern.

2. Pick up a light triangle from the mock-up. Position it, right side up, on the unprinted side of a folded foundation in the corresponding location. The fabric must never extend over any fold line, although it's okay if it doesn't completely cover the seam allowance. Lightly glue the tips of the triangles down. Glue the remaining 2 light triangles in place. You can also use pins if you prefer.

Glue triangles in place.

✻ TIP

Should I use any particular glue stick? It must be washable, not permanent. I prefer Collins Fabric Glue Stick Basting Adhesive. Whatever brand you use, it should go on smoothly. If it leaves clumps of glue, use a fresh glue stick.

✻ TIP

Why do you glue rather than pin? It's simpler! Pins make a small bump in the paper foundation and they just get in the way. However, you can use pins if you prefer.

3. Position the dark triangles as shown and put glue on the two seam allowances at the same time.

Glue the two seam allowances simultaneously.

4. Place the dark triangles, right sides down, on the top of their corresponding light triangles. Glue the dark triangles to the light triangles within the ¼" diagonal seam allowance to secure both the light and dark triangles to the foundation.

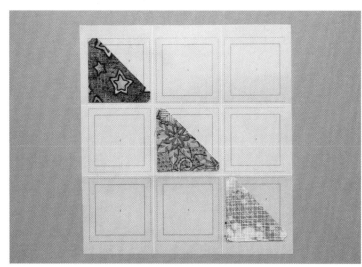

Glue the triangles.

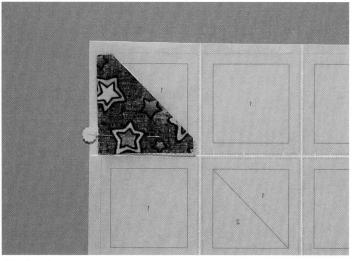

Pinning is an option.

5. Turn the foundation paper over, making sure the pieces didn't shift, and sew a continuous diagonal line through the paper between #1 and #2 to join the triangles. In this instance, you will sew through the seam allowances. Begin and end the stitching beyond the seam allowances at the edge of the block. The beauty of creating any half-square triangle within a block sewn using the Make It Simpler Paper Piecing method is two-fold. It doesn't need to be trued-up, and its diagonal seam is perfectly positioned within the subunit.

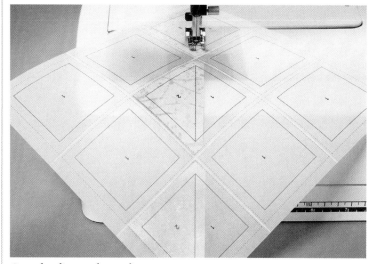

Sew the diagonal seamline.

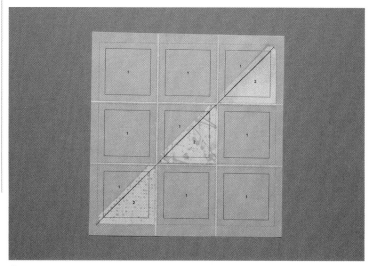

Sewn seam

6. Press the sewn triangles open with an iron (no steam). If your fabric was starched before you began, you can simply finger-press the triangles open.

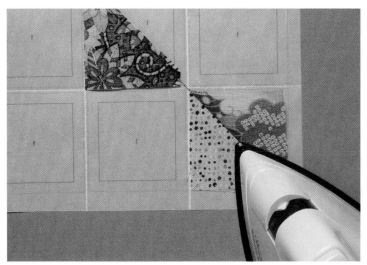

Press the triangle units open.

7. Lightly glue the triangle tips to the paper.

Glue the corners down.

8. Move the 6 fabric squares from the mock-up and lightly glue them in place on the foundation.

Move the squares from the mock-up to the sewing foundation and glue them down.

Joining the Subunits

The 9 subunits are complete. Check to make sure there is no excess fabric lying in the gutter covering a fold line. If so, trim the excess fabric back within the seam allowance. And no pins from here on out!

The subunits are complete.

1. With the fabric side of the foundation face up, fold 1 of the 4 creased lines so that the fabric remains in place, enclosed in the paper, with the printed sewing lines facing you.

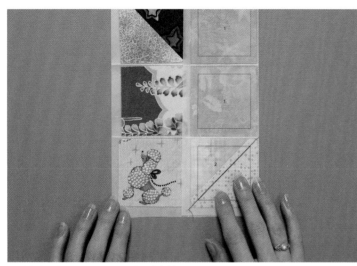

Fold the foundation on the fold line.

2. Begin sewing at the top of the block, at least ⅛" beyond the exterior seam allowance. It's not necessary to backstitch. Sew through this first exterior seam allowance. (Always sew through the exterior seam allowances.) Do not sew through any interior seam allowances.

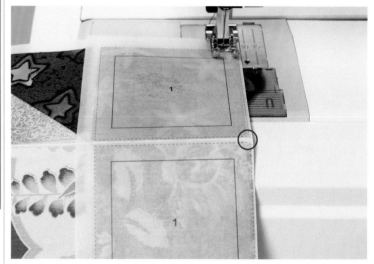

Sew the first seam.

3. Sew along the line of the first #1 square. Stop sewing where the printed line ends. If it is impossible to stop stitching exactly where the printed line ends, it is better to stop stitching a little *before* the end of the line. Raise the needle and presser foot and, without clipping the thread, pass over the first interior seam allowance and lower the needle into the beginning of the printed line of the middle square. Lower the presser foot and continue to sew, raising the needle and passing over each interior seam allowance in the same manner. Continue sewing for at least ⅛" beyond the outside seam allowance line to complete the first seam.

✻ TIP

What are interior and exterior seams?

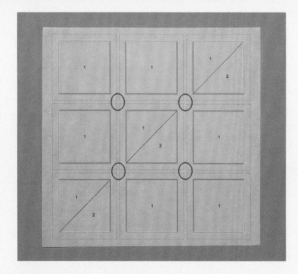

- Interior seams (orange)
- Exterior seams (yellow)
- Interior Seam Allowances (circled)

4. Fold on the creased line parallel to the seam you just sewed, enclosing the fabric again. *Check to be sure the fabric hasn't shifted*, and sew this second seam as you did the first one. Do not sew across any interior seam allowances.

The first seam has been sewn. Sew the second seam.

5. Now that you have sewn both parallel seams, press the seam allowances to the left, then to the right, using a dry iron. Steam can pucker the paper foundation. Use a pressing cloth on top of the printed side of the foundation if the iron melts the printing ink. Make a perpendicular clip at least ⅜" into each of the sewn fold lines. Don't worry: you will be cutting through the loose thread. Nothing bad will happen.

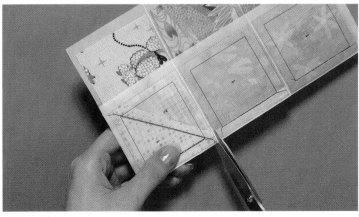

Clip as shown.

6. Fold one of the unsewn sides, enclosing the fabric. It will fold over easily because you snipped the sewn fold lines.

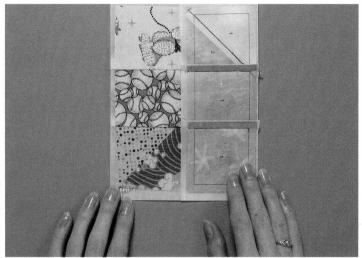

Fold the foundation over, enclosing the fabric.

7. Sew this seam as you did the first seams, but as you approach the seam-allowance "flaps," move them *(on top and underneath)* out of the way of the needle so you don't sew through them. You can backstitch before and after the flap, on the seamline, if you wish.

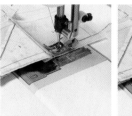 

As you sew the seam, push the flaps out of the way of the needle.

Raise the needle and presser foot, and push the seam-allowance flaps up so you don't sew through them.

Continue stitching.

8. Repeat for the remaining seam. Open your block. Grin. The paper that encases the pair of perpendicular seams may be removed at this time. This allows the block to be pressed very flat. A letter opener is useful for slitting the paper to open the folds. Leave the remaining paper intact until the blocks have been sewn together. Press the seams open or to either side as you see fit, then press the block.

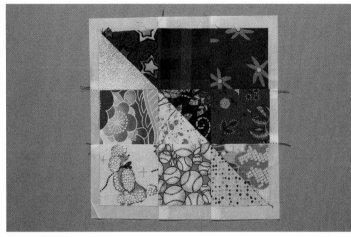

Press the block open.

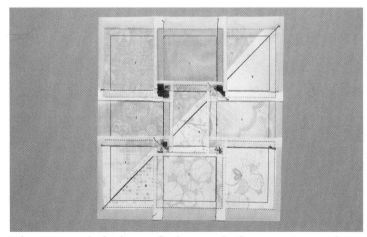

The seams on the back press flat because the flaps weren't sewn down.

9. During the construction of the block, the paper may have decreased in size, and you may find that some seam allowances weren't completely covered by fabric. This is okay. True up the block by centering a 6½" acrylic square on the back of the block (fabric side down), and use it as

a guide to trim the block. Never rely on the printed edge of the foundation as a trimming guide.

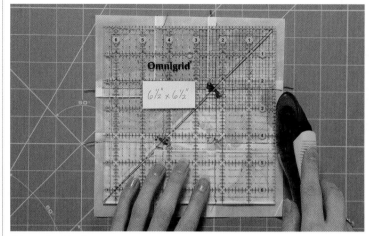

Trim the block.

Finished block (right side)

10. After you have completed all the blocks for your project, join the blocks with a ¼" seam parallel to the edge of the paper. Line the blocks up along the edges of their paper foundations. The fabric may not come out to the edge of the block, so leaving the paper in place gives you an accurate guide for sewing. As you stitch the blocks together, you may remove the paper when you reach an area where you might be sewing more than 2 layers of paper together. You can remove all of the paper after the top has been sewn together.

Ask Anita

1. **What is the most important step to remember?** To first fold and crease the foundation. If you forgot this step before piecing the block, unthread the needle and stitch through the fold line to needle punch the foundation after the fact.

2. **What makes one block easier to make than another?** The easier blocks have one or two pieces per subunit, and fewer seams and intersections.

3. **What makes a block suitable for Make It Simpler paper piecing?** The block needs to have at least one seamline running continuously through it from one side to the other, diagonally, horizontally, or vertically.

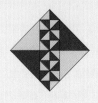

4. **I'm only using two different fabrics in my block. Do I still have to make a mock-up?** Yes, it's a big help. You also might want to make a notation on your foundation as to where each color is placed. Use a permanent pen, because pencil can smudge and ballpoint ink may bleed when ironed.

5. **What is a subunit?** A subunit is a section of the whole block. A block is divided into subunits for construction. After all of the subunits have been assembled, they are joined to make the block. In conventional paper piecing, the subunits are cut apart, pieced, trimmed, and then carefully joined together again. But with my technique, the subunits are never cut apart. With a few folds—no pinning necessary—the subunits come together perfectly. For example, the Nine-Patch Variation (page 8) has 9 subunits, More or Less (page 38) has 4 subunits, the Whirling Hexagon (page 25) has 2 subunits, and the Five-Pointed Star (page 36) has 3 subunits.

6. Can I set up more than one unit at a time? Yes! This is a wonderful time-saver. Set up all the #1 and #2 pieces on the block at the same time. You can even set up more than one block at a time in this manner.

7. What determines piecing order? Piecing order is like mopping the kitchen floor: you don't want to end up in the middle. I have numbered all the blocks with a piecing sequence, but there is often more than one possible way to piece a subunit. I prefer to begin piecing at the perimeter to first cover the edge of the block with fabric, then work toward the center. If I have an especially awkward shape to cover, I will start at that shape if possible. Chinese Lanterns (page 42) and Mill and Star (page 80) blocks work best pieced clockwise or counterclockwise, so their opposing seams fit together. Some patterns with alternate piecing lines, such as the combined More or Less and Mayflower (page 38), take advantage of numbers with letters to distinguish the piecing order.

8. How can I avoid shadowing? When sewing a dark and light fabric together, place the dark fabric on top of the lighter one if possible, then stitch them together. If that's not possible, after sewing, trim back any visible dark fabric in the seam allowance and brush away any dark threads. For example, when two triangles are sewn together to form a subunit in the Nine-Patch Variation block, start by positioning the light fabric, face up. Then, place the dark fabric, face down, on top of it.

9. Is it necessary to cover the seam allowances completely with fabric? No, so long as you end up with at least ⅛" of fabric extending beyond the seam along the edge of the block or between subunits. Conversely, excess fabric on top of the fold between subunits will be a problem when you refold a block. It can push the sewing lines out of alignment. Trim away any fabric that lies over a fold. When the block is squared up, it will be 6½" x 6½". You will sew blocks together using the edge of the paper as your guide, not the fabric.

10. Is there an order to joining the subunits to complete the block? Sew your choice of parallel seams first, whether they are horizontal or vertical. Clip the intersection and then sew the perpendicular seams. Do not sew into the seam allowances (except when they occur at the edge of a block) and do not sew through the flaps that form at perpendicular seams. Doing so makes for bulky intersections, inflexible seams, and more work later to remove small bits of paper. Remember that flaps come in pairs; one on top in plain view and the other underneath, against the feed dogs.

11. What about your "one thread over" trick? When sewing a seam, don't sew right *on* the line, because the stitching takes up space. Your block ends up slightly smaller than it should, and you can lose the tip points. Instead, sew one thread-width over the line into the seam allowance, both when sewing the long seams to join subunits and when sewing blocks into a quilt top. When piecing some subunits (say, sewing piece #2 to piece #1), there is no seam allowance for you to sew "one thread over" into. Instead, sew one thread over into the area that is to be covered by fabric (the area piece #2 is to occupy, and so forth).

12. **Why should I true up my block with a 6½" acrylic square?** Because the foundation may have decreased in size during construction and the printed lines may no longer be accurate guidelines.

13. **Will my rotary cutter become dull from cutting the translucent paper?** Yes. I work with two medium-size rotary cutters, one for paper and one for fabric.

14. **Do I need to stitch the edge of my block once the sewing is complete?** No. If the edge fabric is on the bias or is not lying flat, lightly glue it in place. Extra stitching around the edges makes it harder to remove the paper.

15. **What if I make a mistake and need to rip out a seam?** On the paper side, cover the sewn seam with a piece of Scotch Magic Removable Tape (blue plaid box). Remove the errant stitches from the side opposite the tape, then remove the tape and re-sew the seam with a longer stitch length. *Never* iron a block that has tape on it.

16. **Why should I use a pressing sheet?** Sometimes the toner from the photocopy machine will melt on contact with the iron during pressing and will transfer onto the block. Grrrr. A pressing cloth between your iron and the block will prevent this from happening.

17. **Do you prewash your fabric?** I wash, dry, starch, and iron all of my fabric before use. I like the way it handles after it's been "primed."

18. **Do you ever cut oversized pieces?** Rarely. The ¼" seam allowance is purposely included in the template. It serves as a guideline for positioning adjoining patches and avoids excess fabric in the folded seams. In occasional instances, along the edge of a block, oversize may be advantageous. Note: Pieces that can be cut oversize are indicated by an asterisk on their template.

19. **Can I enlarge the blocks larger than 6"?** No. The patterns fill an 8½" x 11" sheet of paper as they are. Besides, you are limited to the size of translucent paper that a photocopier can accept. *Sometimes the copier will cut off the dashed edge of a foundation pattern, but don't be concerned because the edge isn't used as a trimming guide.*

20. **Do you have any hints for fussy cuts?** Yes. For those pieces cut specifically to feature a motif in the fabric, I photocopy the template onto a sheet of Simple Foundations (available from C&T Publishing). Position the translucent paper template over the fabric and roughly cut out the patch. Reposition the template over the motif on the wrong side of the fabric and lightly glue-baste the template in place for an accurate guide. Rotary cut the shape out using an Omnigrid ruler for a straightedge. If you need to cut a reverse patch, simply turn the template over.

LEGEND

◻ Cut a square the size indicated on the template pattern, then cut diagonally in half to yield half-square triangles.

⊠ Cut a square the size indicated on the template pattern, then cut it diagonally twice to yield quarter-square triangles.

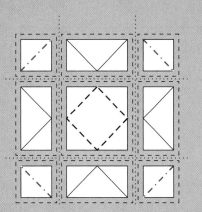

Fold line ·····················

Outside line - - - - - - - - - - - -

Design line for alternate block in multiple block pattern · - · - · - · - · - · - ·

Design line for alternate block in multiple block pattern - - - - - - - - - -

Design line for alternate block in multiple block pattern

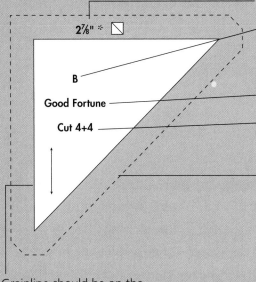

2⅞" ∗ ◻

B

Good Fortune

Cut 4+4

Square size from which this triangle is cut

Template letter on the block diagram
A=Template A, AR=Template A Reversed
(turned face down on fabric)

Name of the block

How many light and dark triangles to cut

Template pattern—use to ensure pattern coverage, but not too large

Grainline should be on the straight of the grain.

Denotes that this patch may be cut oversize.
∗∗ Denotes that this measurement is slightly smaller than the pattern. Cut to the size indicated. The tip will be blunted for ease in block construction.

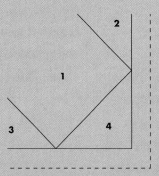

Sequential piecing order

SUPPLY LIST

#90/14 needles	Matching thread	Scotch Magic Removable Tape
Collins fabric gluestick	Omnigrid 6½" square ruler	Seam ripper
Fabric	Paper scissors	Sewing machine
Fabric scissors	Photocopier paper	Spray starch
Iron	Pins (optional)	Translucent paper (Simple
Letter opener	Pressing cloth	Foundations)
Lightbox (optional)	Rotary cutter and mat	

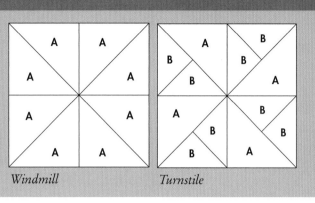

Windmill   *Turnstile*

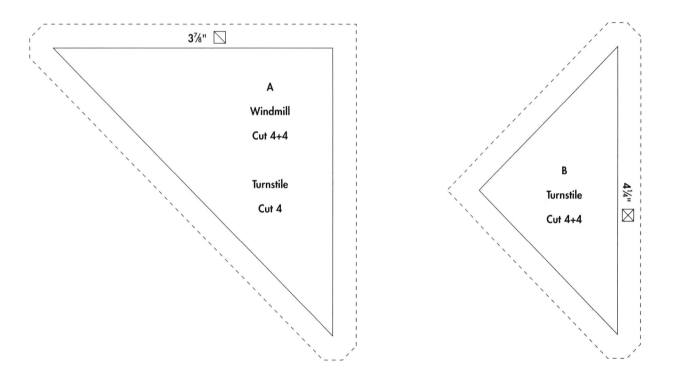

3⅞" ◸

A

Windmill

Cut 4+4

Turnstile

Cut 4

B

Turnstile

Cut 4+4

4¼" ⊠

HELPFUL HINTS

To avoid bulk, don't stitch past the inner parallel seamlines. Once the two subunits are sewn together, all the fabric patches will be secured and you can press the seam open.

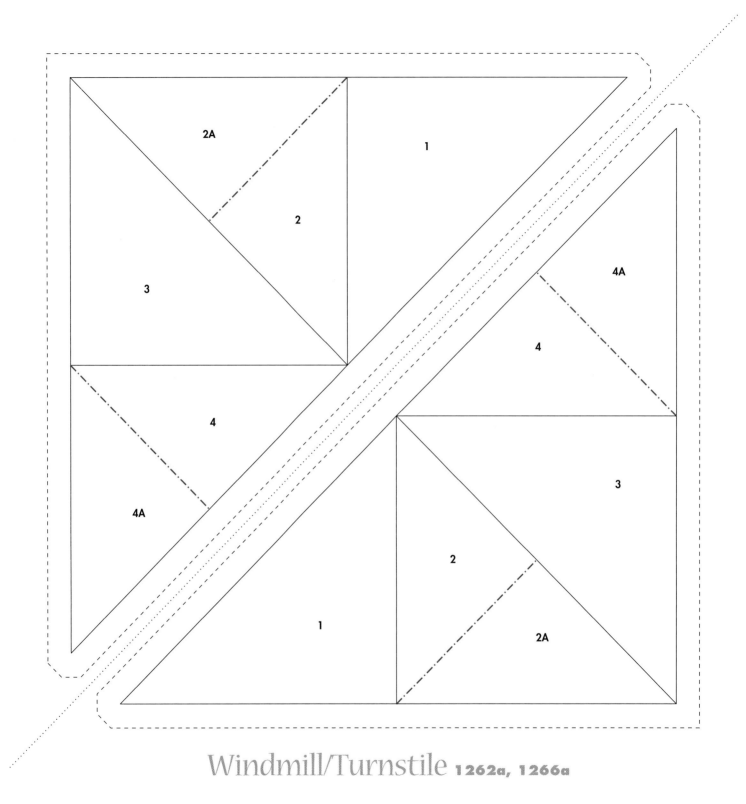

Windmill/Turnstile **1262a, 1266a**

Whirling Hexagon 245 (modified)

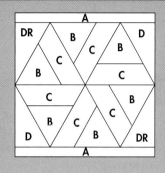

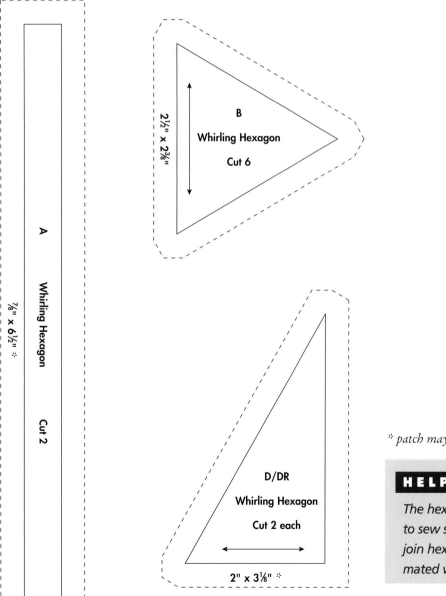

A

Whirling Hexagon

Cut 2

7/8" x 6½" *

B

Whirling Hexagon

Cut 6

2½" x 2⅜"

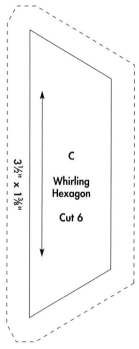

C

Whirling Hexagon

Cut 6

3½" x 1⅜"

D/DR

Whirling Hexagon

Cut 2 each

2" x 3⅛" *

* patch may be cut oversize

HELPFUL HINTS

The hexagon is set within a square. It's simpler to sew squares together than it would be to join hexagons together. The quilt appears animated with hexagon stick figures.

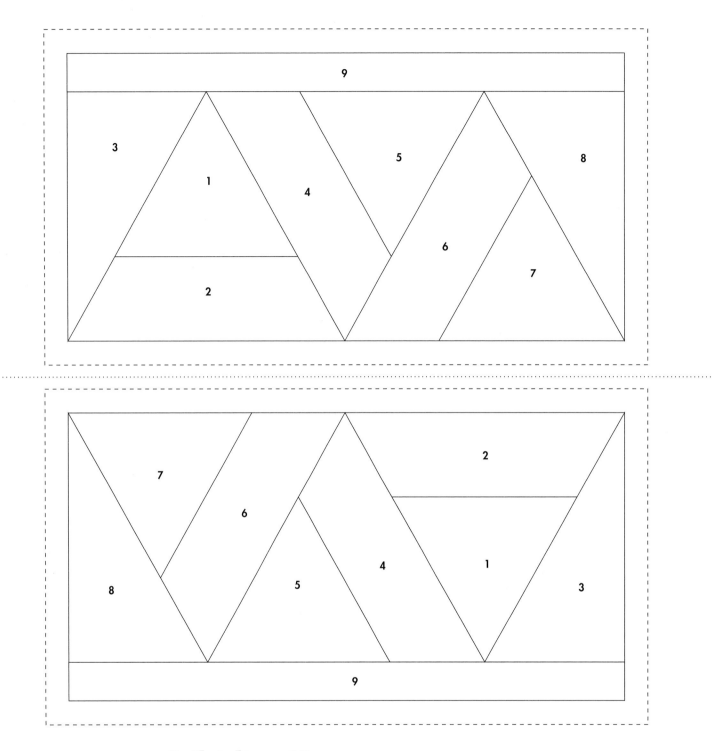

Whirling Hexagon 245 (modified)

Whirling Hexagon

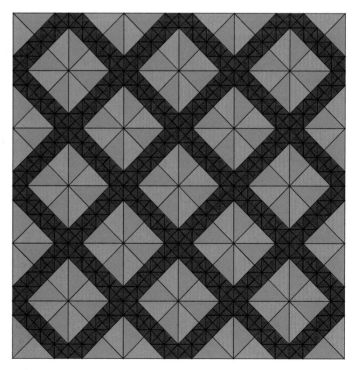

Starry Path

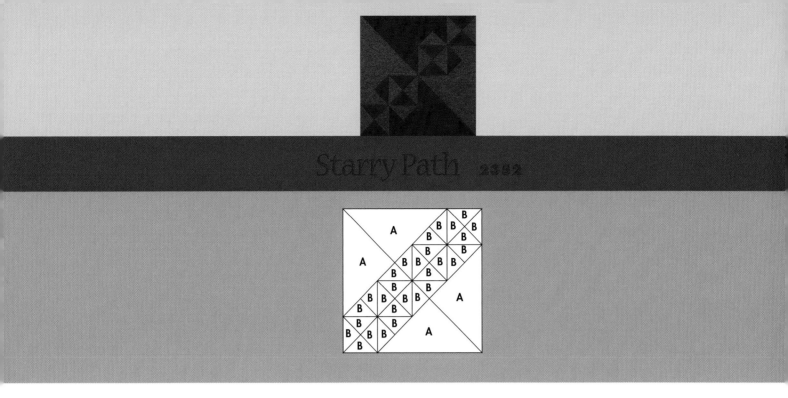

Starry Path 2382

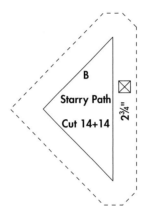

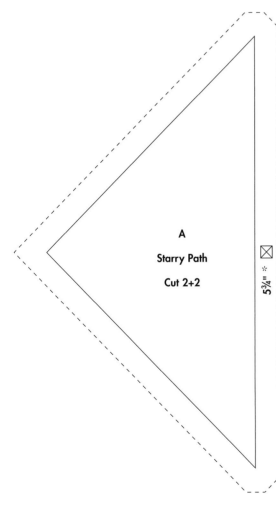

A

Starry Path

Cut 2+2

5¾" *

B

Starry Path

Cut 14+14

2¾"

* patch may be cut oversize

HELPFUL HINTS

This is an easy and straightforward block. Precut all of the small triangles to the exact shape of the small triangle template. Glue each of the four #1 triangles to the foundation right side up. Add the #2 triangles and continue to piece in this assembly-line manner.

Because the triangles are cut to size, each new triangle is aligned along the edge of the triangle that preceded it. It's always a good idea to check your work from the back as you piece, just to be sure the sewn triangles are extending ¼" beyond the seamline. If they aren't, make an adjustment when adding the next piece. Finger-press or use an iron after each successive group of triangles is added, and lightly glue the pressed triangles in place to keep them from slipping when the next triangle is added. You may wish to cut the large triangles oversize.

Starry Path 2352

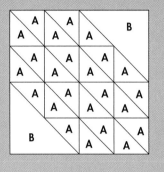

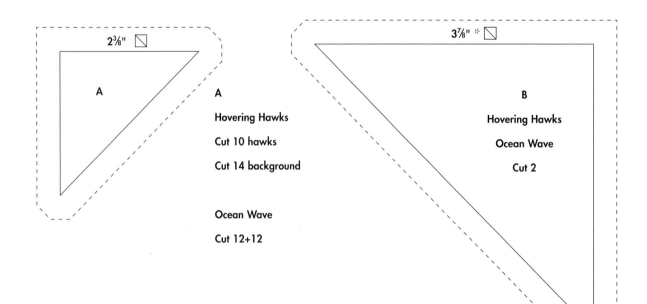

2⅜"

A

A

Hovering Hawks

Cut 10 hawks

Cut 14 background

Ocean Wave

Cut 12+12

3⅞" ∗

B

Hovering Hawks

Ocean Wave

Cut 2

∗ patch may be cut oversize

HELPFUL HINTS

It's interesting that both of these blocks have the same architecture, but fabric placement defines them. Four of the Ocean Wave quarter blocks must be joined to make a complete Ocean Wave block.

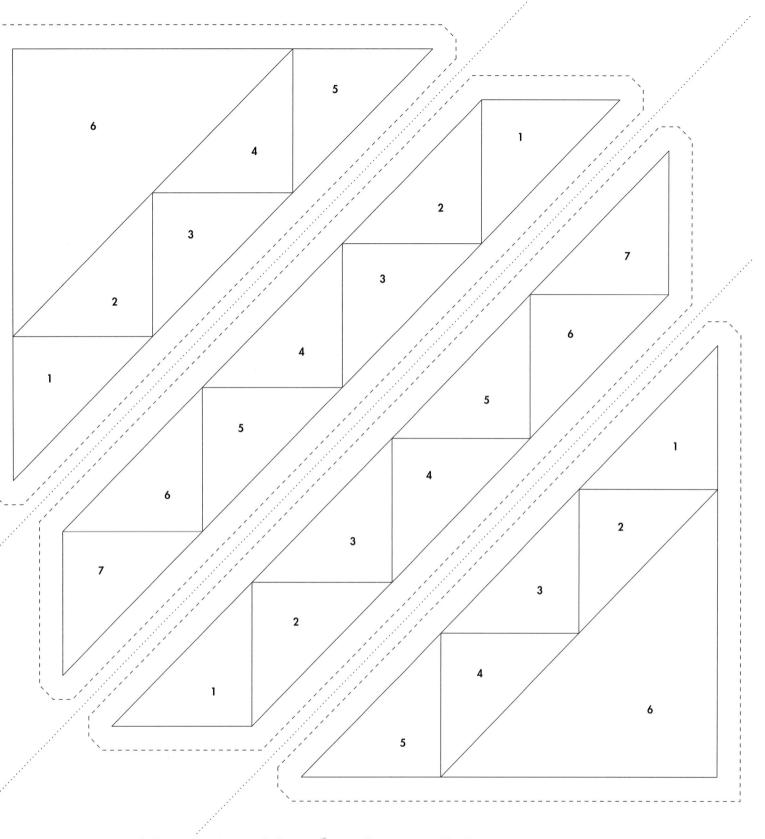

Hovering Hawks, Ocean Wave 1323, 283

Hovering Hawks

Ocean Wave

Necktie 1376

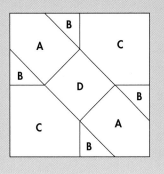

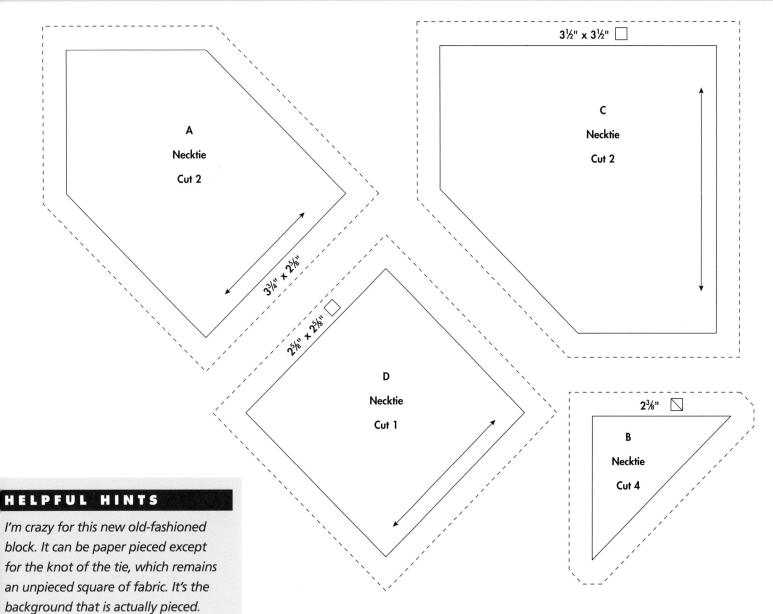

A
Necktie
Cut 2

3¾" x 2⅝"

3½" x 3½" ▢

C
Necktie
Cut 2

2⅝" x 2⅝" ▢

D
Necktie
Cut 1

2⅜" ◹

B
Necktie
Cut 4

HELPFUL HINTS

I'm crazy for this new old-fashioned block. It can be paper pieced except for the knot of the tie, which remains an unpieced square of fabric. It's the background that is actually pieced.

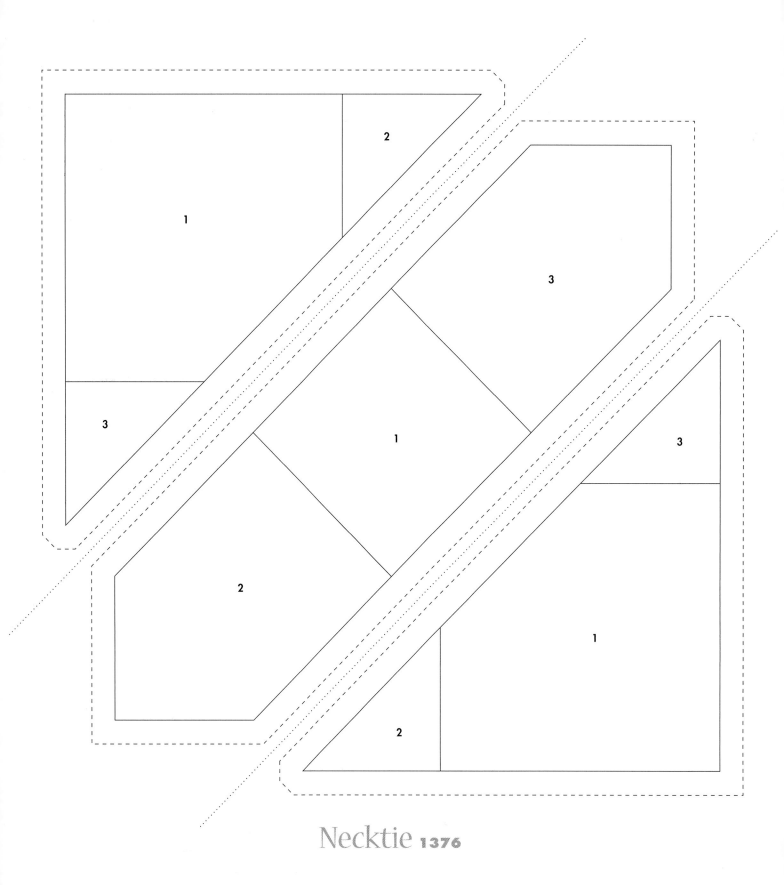

Necktie 1376

Necktie

by Susan Stauber, New York, NY

Five Points on Leave

by Constance Benson and Denise Bradley, New York, NY

Five-Pointed Star U004 (modified)

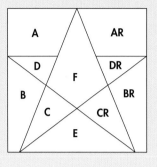

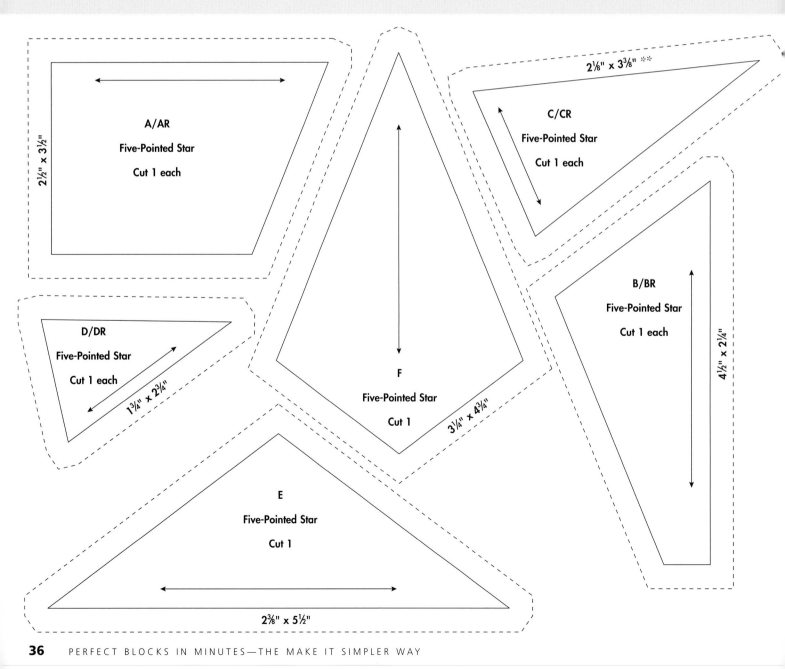

A/AR
Five-Pointed Star
Cut 1 each

$2\frac{1}{2}$" x $3\frac{1}{2}$"

$2\frac{1}{8}$" x $3\frac{3}{8}$" ✳✳

C/CR
Five-Pointed Star
Cut 1 each

D/DR
Five-Pointed Star
Cut 1 each

$1\frac{3}{4}$" x $2\frac{3}{4}$"

B/BR
Five-Pointed Star
Cut 1 each

$4\frac{1}{2}$" x $2\frac{1}{4}$"

F
Five-Pointed Star
Cut 1

$3\frac{1}{4}$" x $4\frac{3}{4}$"

E
Five-Pointed Star
Cut 1

$2\frac{3}{8}$" x $5\frac{1}{2}$"

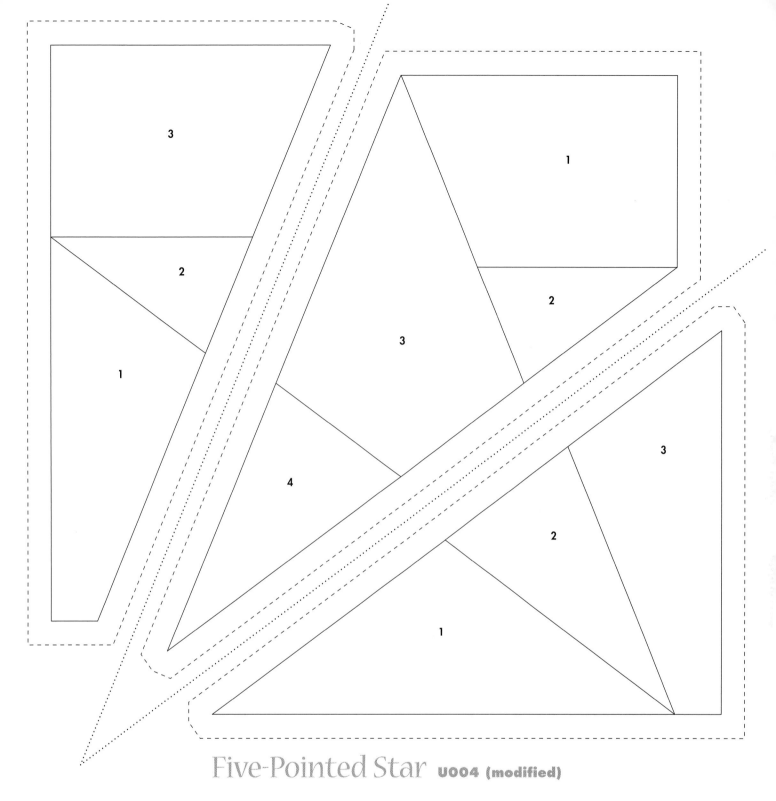

Five-Pointed Star U004 (modified)

** *This measurement is slightly smaller than the pattern. Cut to the size indicated. The tip will be blunted for ease in block construction.*

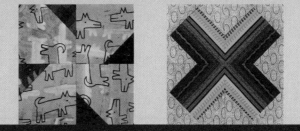

More or Less, The Mayflower (modified)

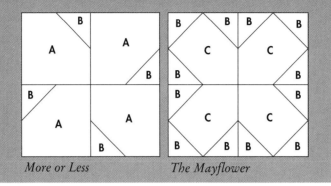

More or Less   *The Mayflower*

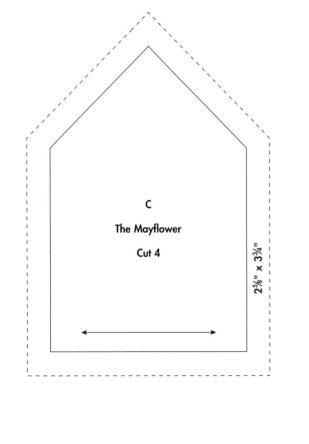

C

The Mayflower

Cut 4

2⅝" x 3¾"

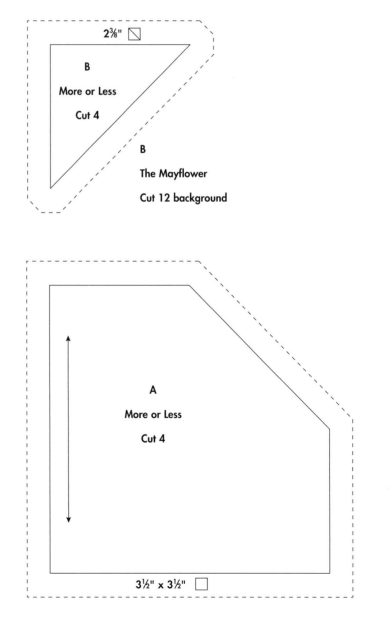

2⅜"

B

More or Less

Cut 4

B

The Mayflower

Cut 12 background

A

More or Less

Cut 4

3½" x 3½"

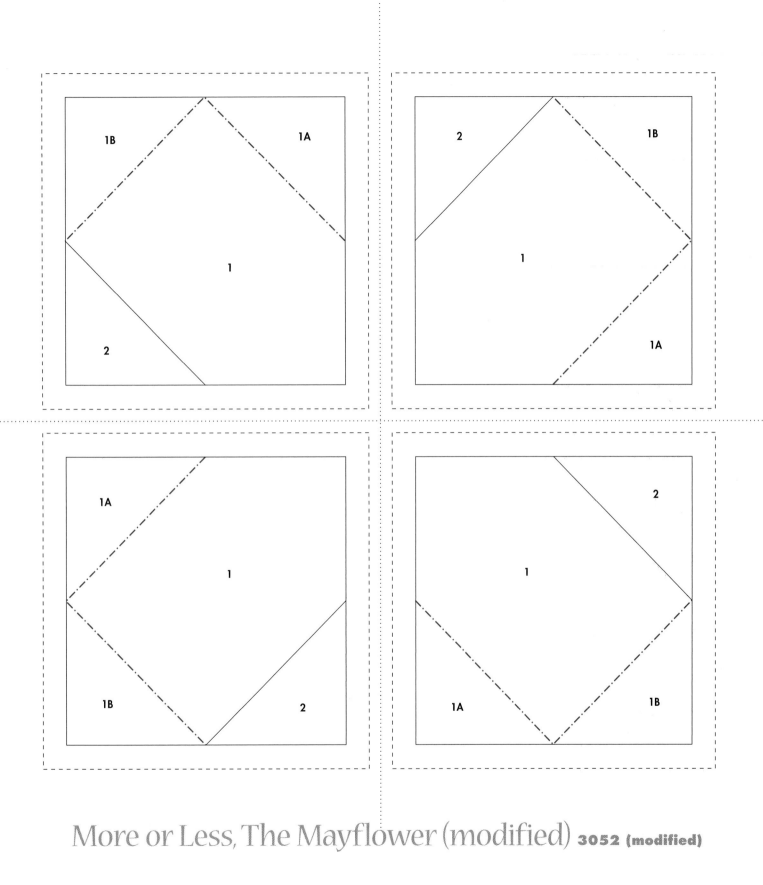

More or Less, The Mayflower (modified) 3052 (modified)

For each More or Less block, cut four 3½" squares from the one fabric and trim using the A template. Glue the A pieces in place. Cut four B pieces from the same fabric as the A pieces. Stack and pin the four triangles to the foundation for later use. Repeat for all the foundations and arrange them into position for the quilt top.

Stay organized. Mark each foundation paper. Use a fabric pen so your notes will be dark enough to read and won't smear when ironed. Write on the front (fabric side) to avoid turning the blocks over. Note the top of each block with an up arrow and the position of each block in the layout, such as A1, B1, A2. Sew the reserved triangles to the adjoining blocks to create the tessellated blocks.

Template tricks: Template C is the trimming guide for the modified Mayflower. These illustrations show striped fabric that was folded to yield matching pairs.

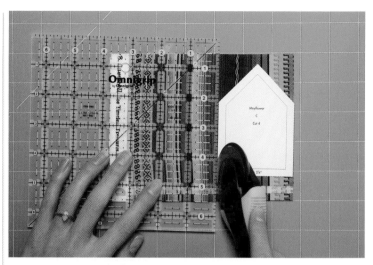

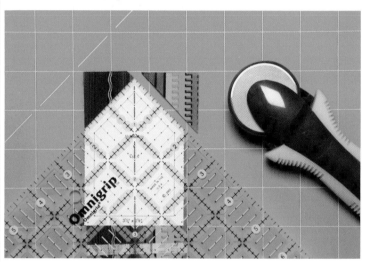

Trim around the template.

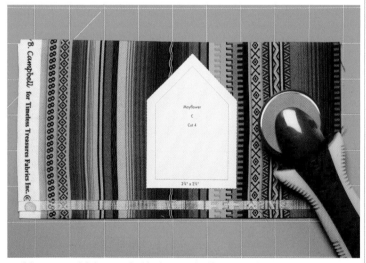

Fold a strip of fabric in half, then in half again, aligning one particular stripe on all four layers. Position template (copied onto translucent vellum), and glue-baste in place (optional).

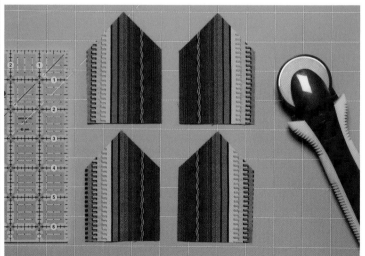

Pairs of mirrored pieces ready for the Mayflower

More or Less

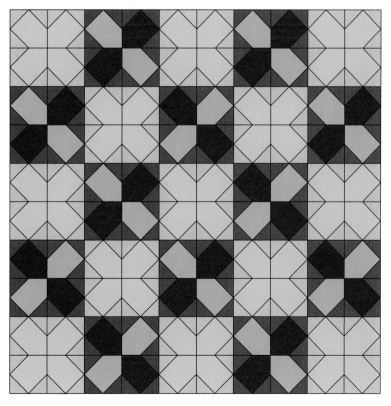

The Mayflower

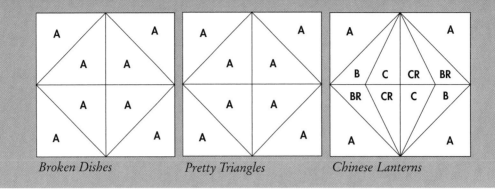

Broken Dishes   Pretty Triangles   Chinese Lanterns

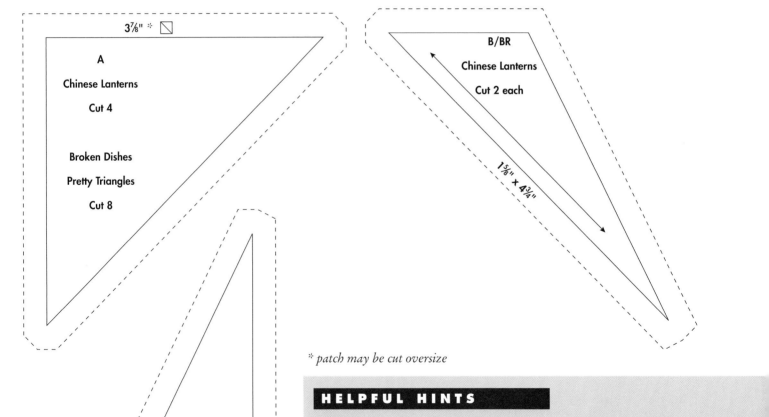

3⅞" *

A

Chinese Lanterns

Cut 4

Broken Dishes

Pretty Triangles

Cut 8

B/BR

Chinese Lanterns

Cut 2 each

1⅝" x 4¾"

C/CR

Chinese Lanterns

Cut 2 each

2" x 3½"

* patch may be cut oversize

HELPFUL HINTS

The background of Chinese Lanterns is made from four half-square triangles. The block is pieced in a clockwise manner so the seams will lie adjacent to one another. The other two blocks are each made entirely from eight half-square triangles. Broken Dishes calls for two different fabrics, while Pretty Triangles makes use of eight different fabrics. When sewing the pairs of triangles for Broken Dishes and Pretty Triangles, the lighter fabric of the pair should be glued in place, right side up. As with all subunits of only two triangles, the darker of the two is placed and sewn right side down on top of the lighter one, regardless of the printed piecing order.

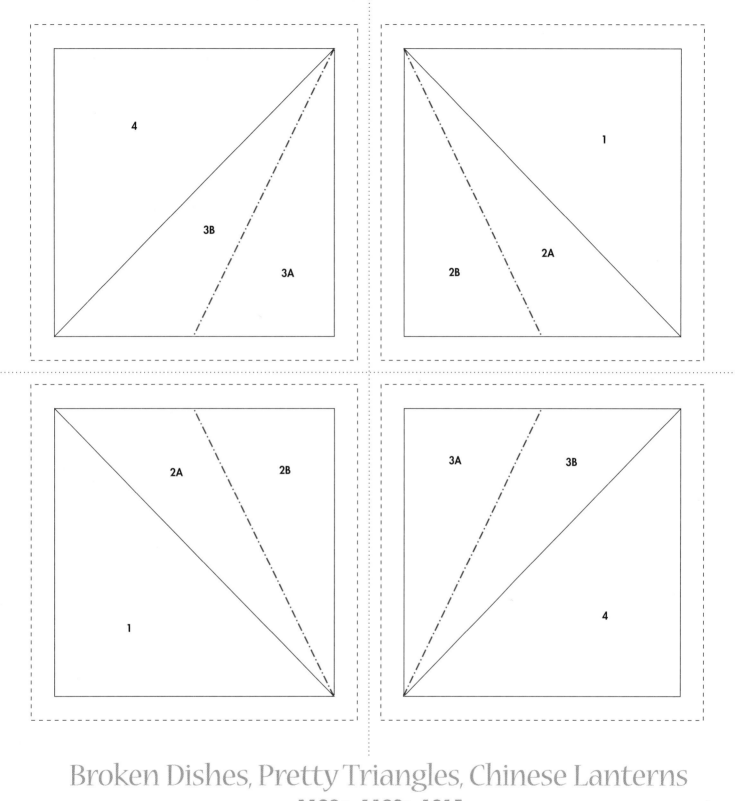

Broken Dishes, Pretty Triangles, Chinese Lanterns
1193a, 1193c, 1215

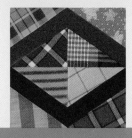

Left and Right 1188

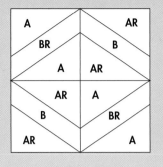

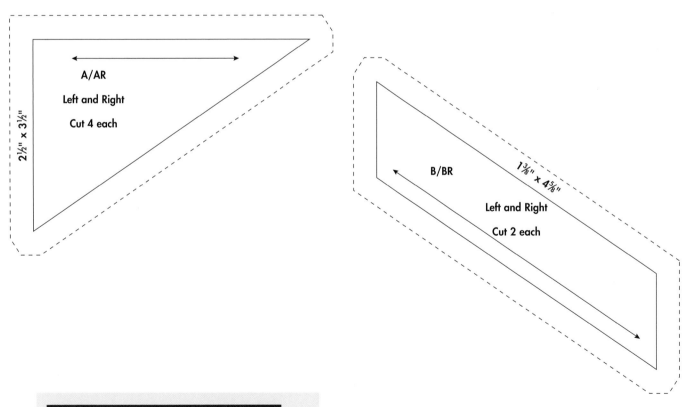

A/AR

Left and Right

Cut 4 each

2½" x 3½"

B/BR

1⅜" x 4⅝"

Left and Right

Cut 2 each

HELPFUL HINTS

This block is pieced in a clockwise order. The seams of the narrow diagonal strips will nest.

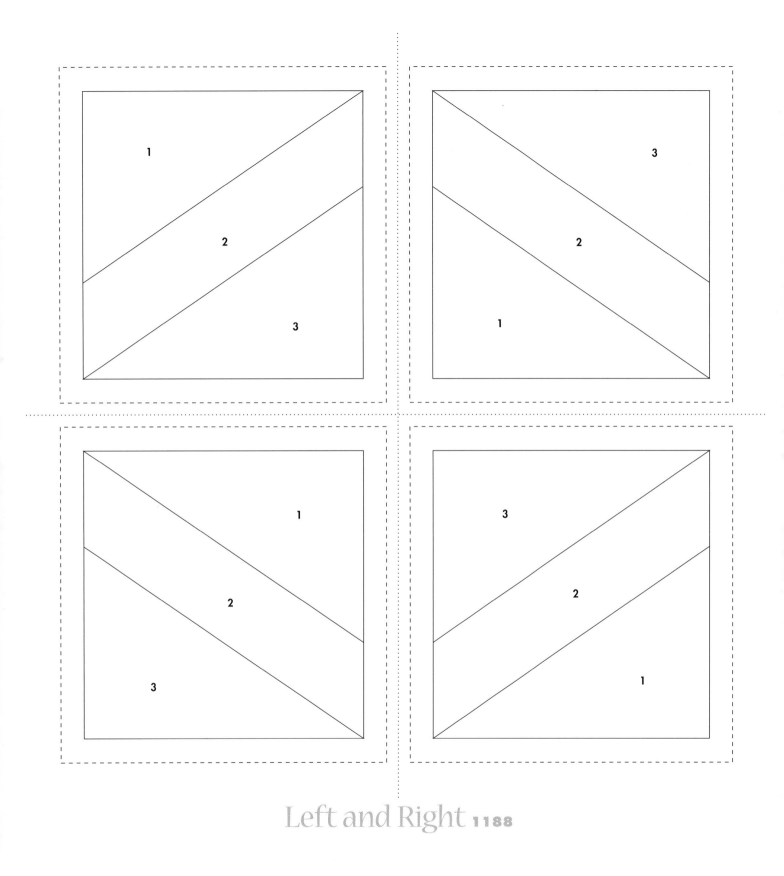

Left and Right 1188

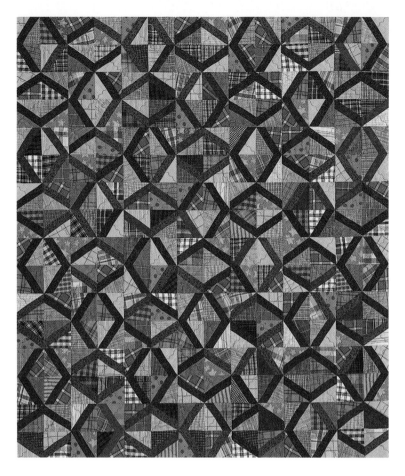

Left and Right
by Susan Stauber, New York, NY

Birds in the Air
by Pamela Creason, Christine Taylor, and
Andrea Verzantvoort, Pleasanton, CA

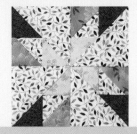

Birds in the Air

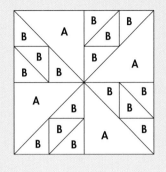

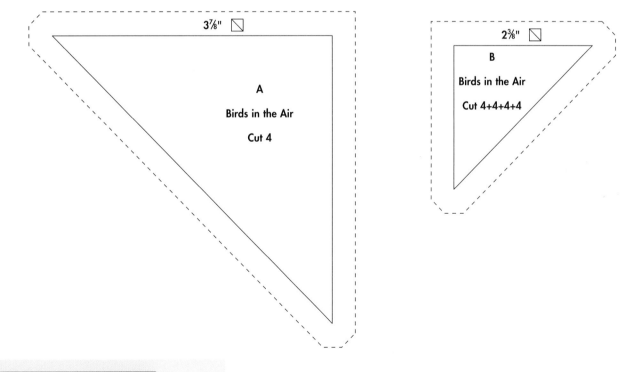

3⅞" ▢

A

Birds in the Air

Cut 4

2⅜" ▢

B

Birds in the Air

Cut 4+4+4+4

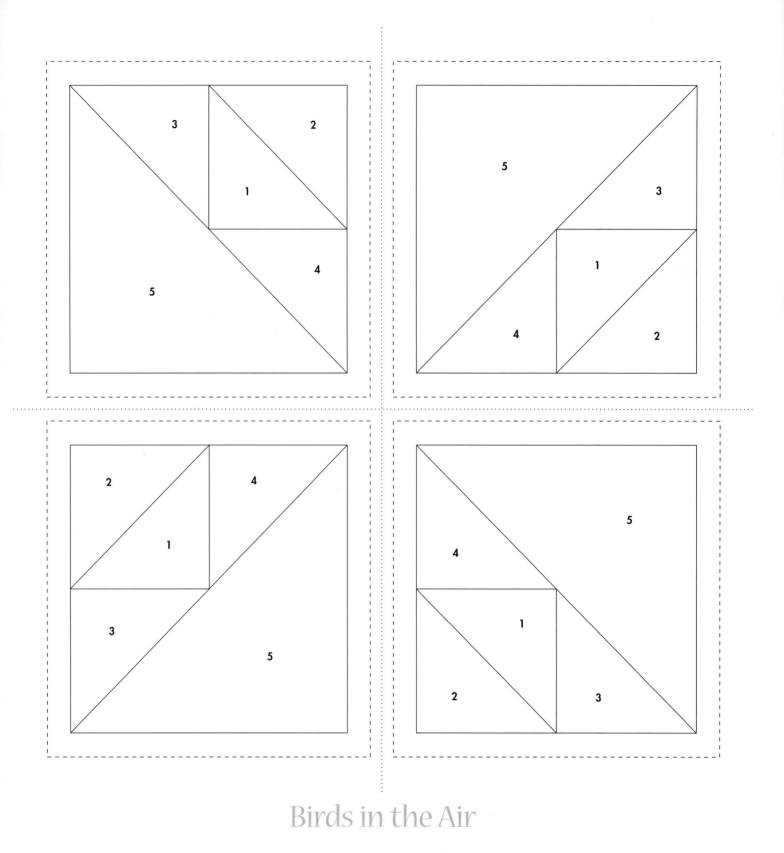

Birds in the Air

Endless Chain 2716 (modified)

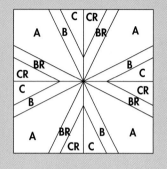

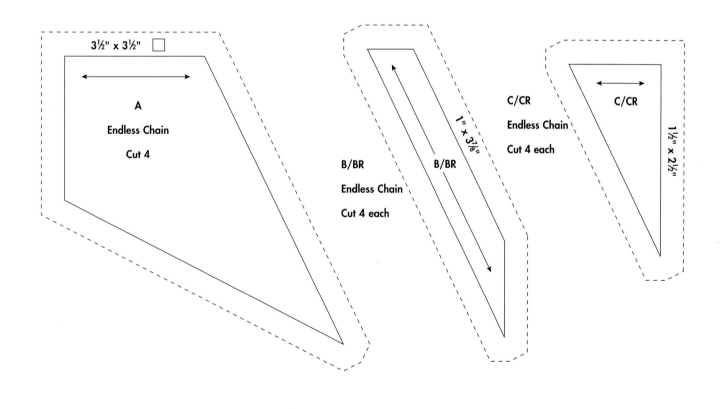

3½" x 3½"

A

Endless Chain

Cut 4

B/BR

Endless Chain

Cut 4 each

1" x 3⅞"

C/CR

Endless Chain

Cut 4 each

1½" x 2½"

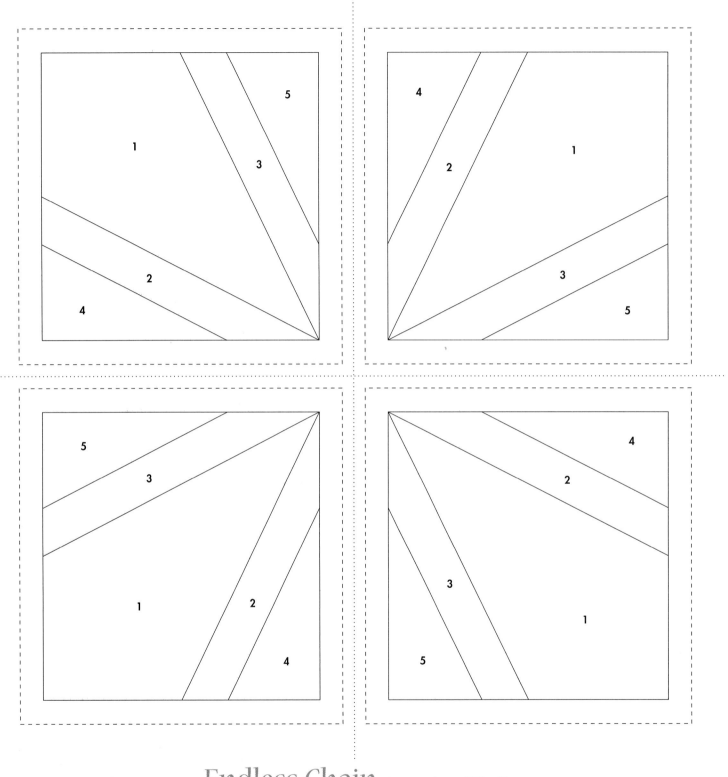

Endless Chain 2716 (modified)

Endless Chain

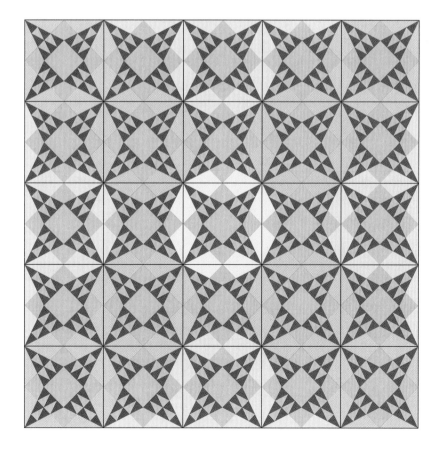

Pine Burr Wedding Ring

Pine Burr 1253 (modified)

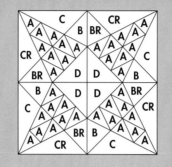

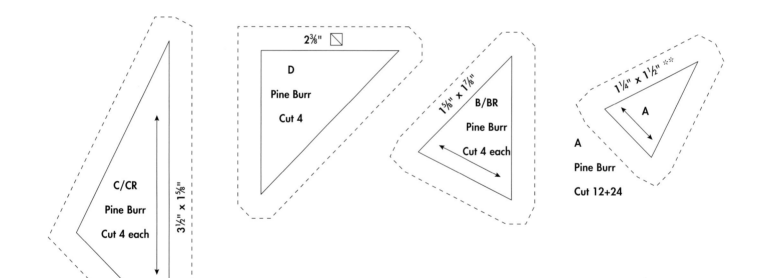

2⅜" ▱

D

Pine Burr

Cut 4

1⅝" x 1⅞"

B/BR

Pine Burr

Cut 4 each

1¼" x 1½" **

A

A

Pine Burr

Cut 12+24

3½" x 1⅝"

C/CR

Pine Burr

Cut 4 each

** *This measurement is slightly smaller than the pattern. Cut to the size indicated. The tip will be blunted for ease in block construction.*

HELPFUL HINTS

When a template indicates cutting a reverse, such as B/BR, it's also an indicator that the shape, even if it doesn't look like it, is asymmetrical.

Pine Burr 1253 (modified)

Nine-Patch, Wild Geese, Simplex Star, Double Hour Glass, Hour Glass

1601a, 1692b, 1717, 1687a, 1705

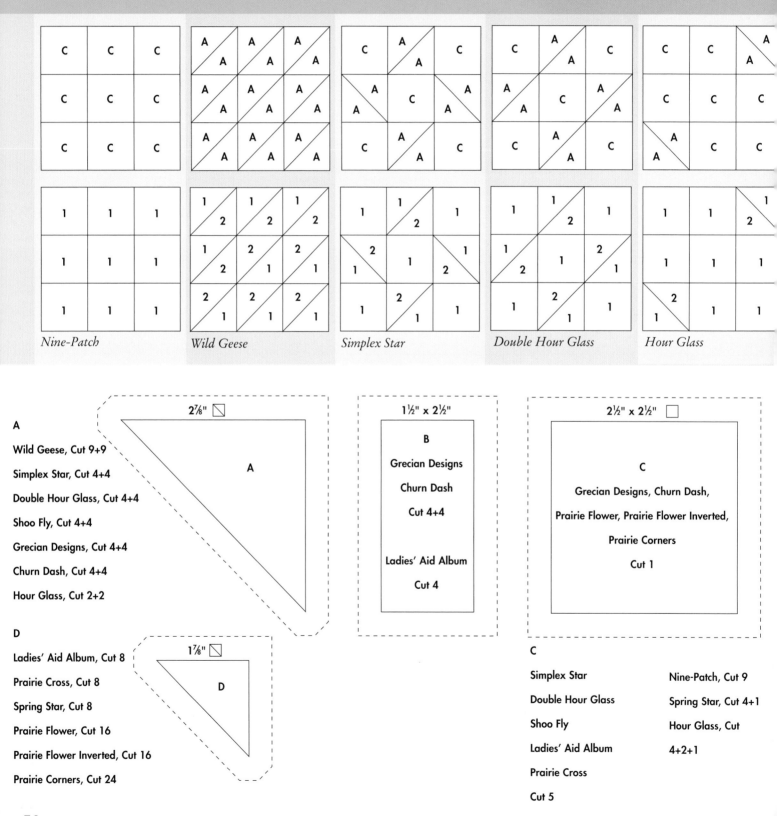

Nine-Patch   *Wild Geese*   *Simplex Star*   *Double Hour Glass*   *Hour Glass*

A

Wild Geese, Cut 9+9

Simplex Star, Cut 4+4

Double Hour Glass, Cut 4+4

Shoo Fly, Cut 4+4

Grecian Designs, Cut 4+4

Churn Dash, Cut 4+4

Hour Glass, Cut 2+2

2⅞" A

D

Ladies' Aid Album, Cut 8

Prairie Cross, Cut 8

Spring Star, Cut 8

Prairie Flower, Cut 16

Prairie Flower Inverted, Cut 16

Prairie Corners, Cut 24

1⅞" D

1½" x 2½"

B

Grecian Designs

Churn Dash

Cut 4+4

Ladies' Aid Album

Cut 4

2½" x 2½"

C

Grecian Designs, Churn Dash,

Prairie Flower, Prairie Flower Inverted,

Prairie Corners

Cut 1

C

Simplex Star

Double Hour Glass

Shoo Fly

Ladies' Aid Album

Prairie Cross

Cut 5

Nine-Patch, Cut 9

Spring Star, Cut 4+1

Hour Glass, Cut

4+2+1

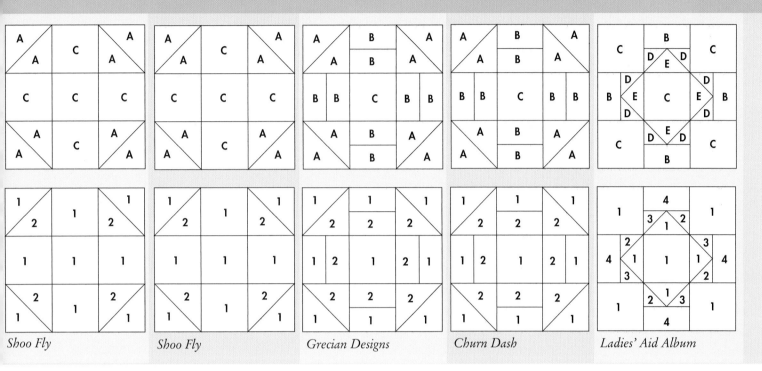

Shoo Fly   Shoo Fly   Grecian Designs   Churn Dash   Ladies' Aid Album

s measurement is slightly smaller than the pattern. Cut to the size indicated. The tip will be blunted for ease in block construction.

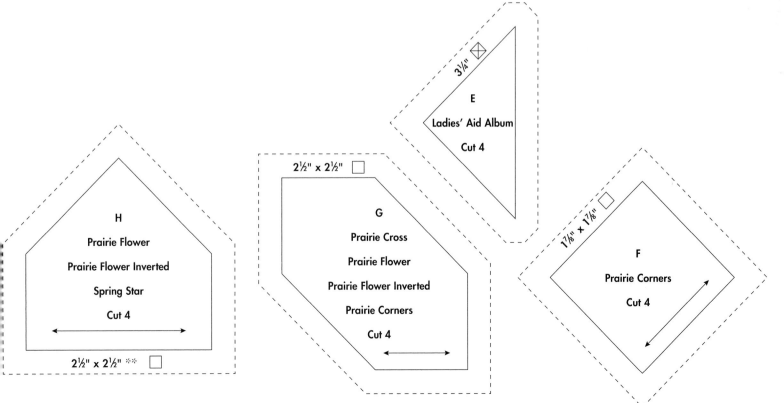

H

Prairie Flower

Prairie Flower Inverted

Spring Star

Cut 4

2½" x 2½" ✳✳ ☐

G

Prairie Cross

Prairie Flower

Prairie Flower Inverted

Prairie Corners

Cut 4

2½" x 2½" ☐

E

Ladies' Aid Album

Cut 4

3¼" ◈

F

Prairie Corners

Cut 4

1⅞" x 1⅞" ☐

Prairie Cross; Prairie Flower; Prairie Flower, Inverted; Prairie Corners; Spring St...

1755 (modified) all

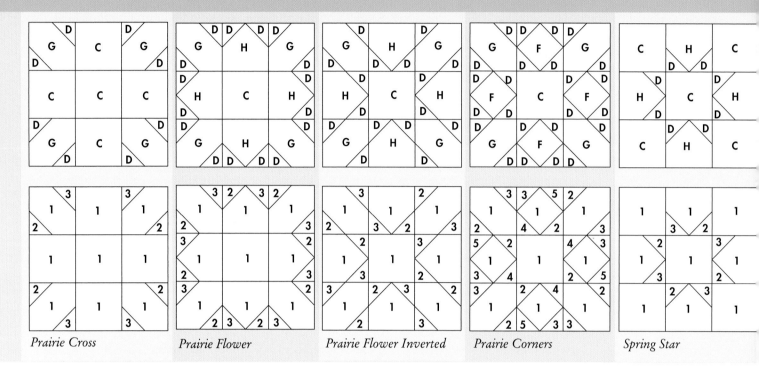

Prairie Cross   Prairie Flower   Prairie Flower Inverted   Prairie Corners   Spring Star

HELPFUL HINTS

Nine-Patch family blocks are simple to construct. There are only four folds and many have minimal piecing. The basic Nine-Patch is nine squares of fabric glued rather than sewn to the foundation, making them suitable for children to sew. A simple quilt setting would alternate a dark block (5 dark patches/4 light patches) with a light one (5 light patches/4 dark ones) for a checkerboard effect.

The fourteen blocks are divided into two groups: the Nine-Patch family and the Prairie Flower family. The Nine-Patch family blocks can be pieced on the Nine-Patch Multiple Pattern. The four Prairie blocks share the Prairie Family and Spring Star Multiple Pattern with the Spring Star. Refer to the small diagrams of each block for fabric placement and sewing order. Once the pieces have been cut and a mock-up made, it should become clear as to which piecing lines are to be sewn. There are many Nine-Patch family blocks in existence. Treat these multiple-block patterns as worksheets and make foundations for other blocks that interest you by adapting the design lines as needed.

Here is a piecing shortcut for blocks with patches in continuous diagonal lines, such as the triangles in Wild Geese, Double Hour Glass and Prairie Corners. Sew pairs of triangles together, then continue sewing, without lifting the needle, through the seam allowances to the next pair of patches. Sewing through the seam allowance is permissible because you are sewing through only a single layer of paper, not joining subunits.

Nine-Patch Family Multiple Pattern

1601a, 1692b, 1717, 1687a, 1705, 1645, 1645, 1646b, 1646a, 1719

Prairie Family and Spring Star Multiple Pattern 1755 (modified)

Spring Star
by Janice E. Petre, Sinking Spring, PA

Prairie Home Companion
by Marcella Peek, Belmont, CA

Double Hour Glass

by the Riverbank Quilters, New York, NY

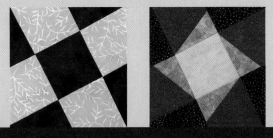

Washington's Puzzle, Delaware Crosspatch 2562, 2563

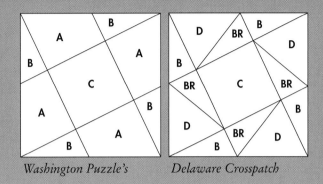

Washington Puzzle's   *Delaware Crosspatch*

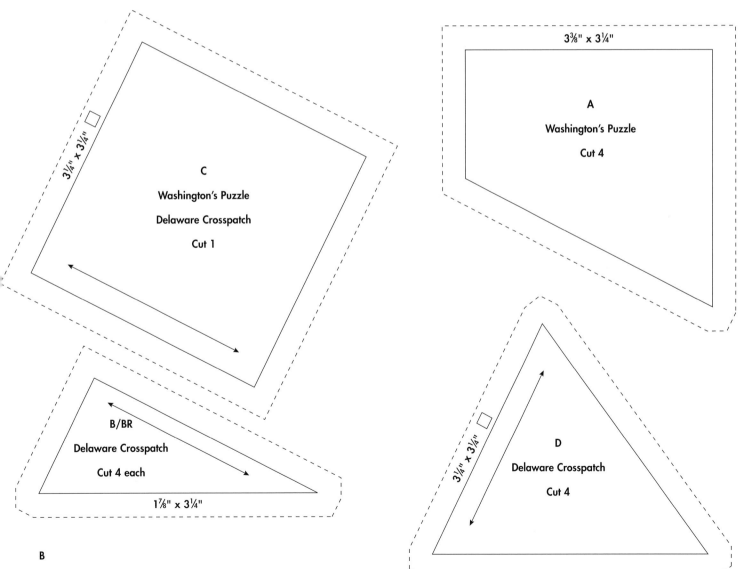

3⅜" x 3¼"

A

Washington's Puzzle

Cut 4

3¼" x 3¼"

C

Washington's Puzzle

Delaware Crosspatch

Cut 1

B/BR

Delaware Crosspatch

Cut 4 each

1⅞" x 3¼"

3¼" x 3¼"

D

Delaware Crosspatch

Cut 4

B

Washington's Puzzle

Cut 4

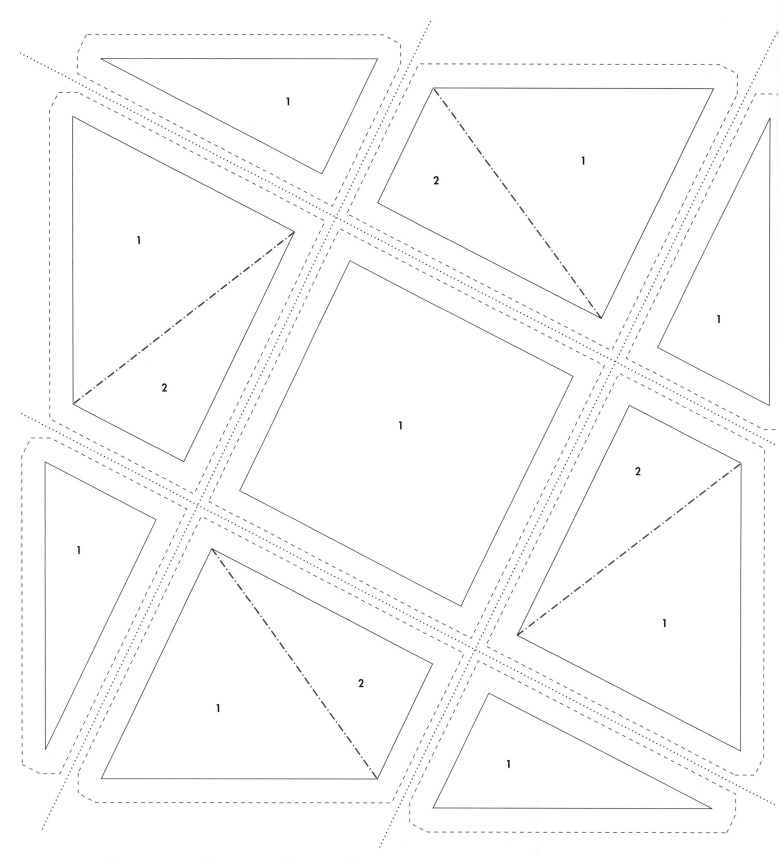

Washington's Puzzle, Delaware Crosspatch 2562, 2563

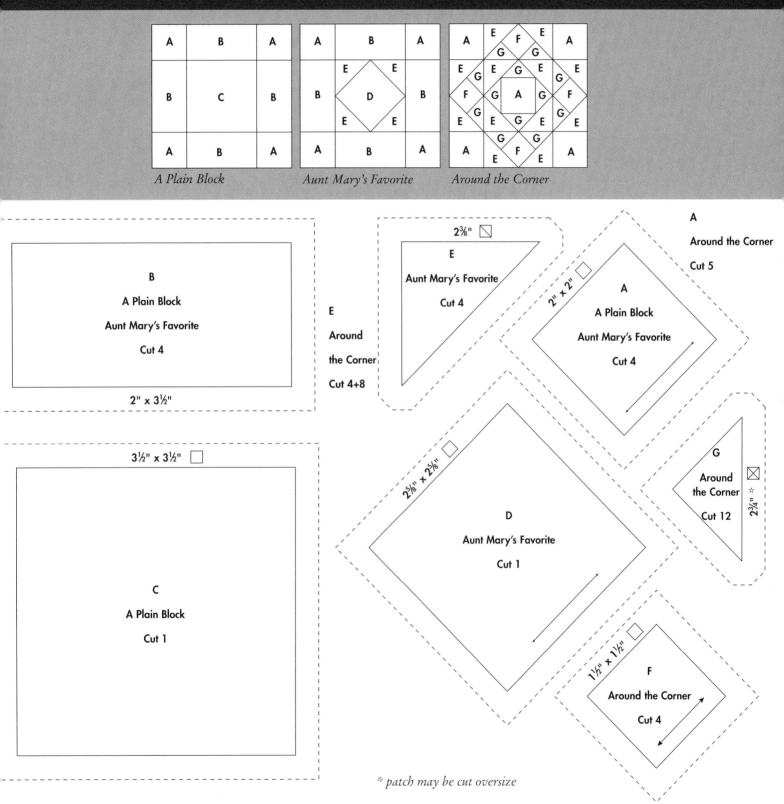

A Plain Block *Aunt Mary's Favorite* *Around the Corner*

B

A Plain Block

Aunt Mary's Favorite

Cut 4

2" x 3½"

E

Around

the Corner

Cut 4+8

2⅜"

E

Aunt Mary's Favorite

Cut 4

A

Around the Corner

Cut 5

2" x 2"

A

A Plain Block

Aunt Mary's Favorite

Cut 4

3½" x 3½"

C

A Plain Block

Cut 1

G

Around

the Corner

Cut 12

2¾" *

2⅝" x 2⅝"

D

Aunt Mary's Favorite

Cut 1

1½" x 1½"

F

Around the Corner

Cut 4

* patch may be cut oversize

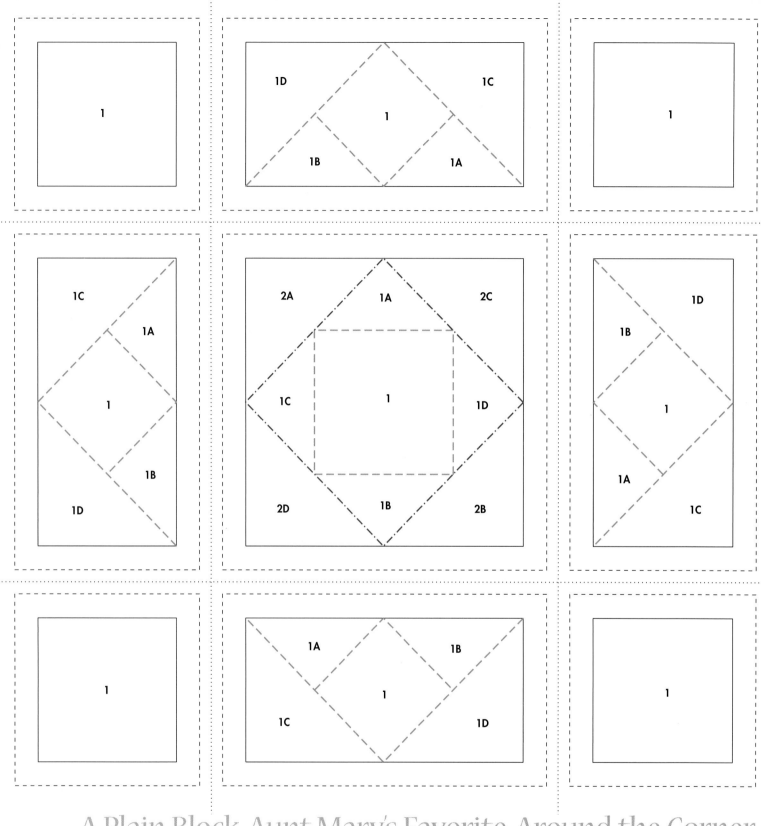

A Plain Block, Aunt Mary's Favorite, Around the Corner

2020, K022, 2043

HELPFUL HINTS

Assembly-line piece Around the Corner whenever possible. For the pieced center, sew two opposite triangles within the subunit rather than sewing one triangle at a time. Turn over, press, position the next pair, and sew. In the outer rectangular subunits, glue all four F squares in place. Place the first of the adjoining triangles in position 1A in each subunit and sew them before turning the foundation to the front to press and prepare for the consecutive go-rounds of triangles. Last, glue the corner squares in position and join the subunits.

Celebration

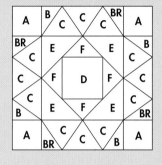

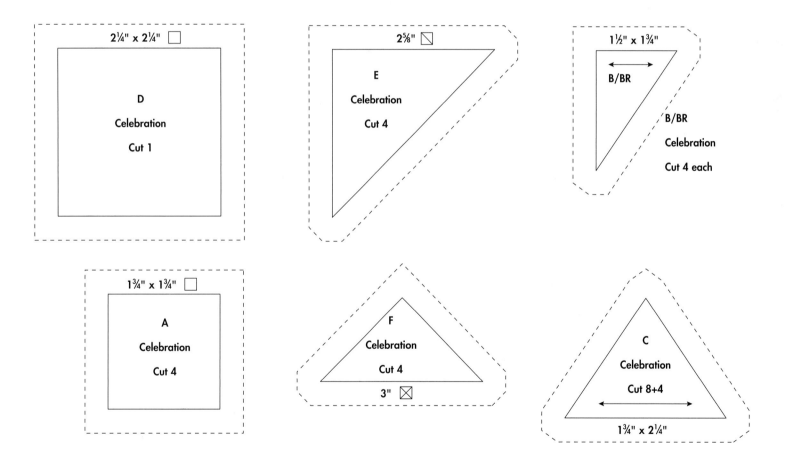

2¼" x 2¼" □

D

Celebration

Cut 1

2⅝" ◿

E

Celebration

Cut 4

1½" x 1¾"

B/BR

B/BR

Celebration

Cut 4 each

1¾" x 1¾" □

A

Celebration

Cut 4

F

Celebration

Cut 4

3" ⊠

C

Celebration

Cut 8+4

1¾" x 2¼"

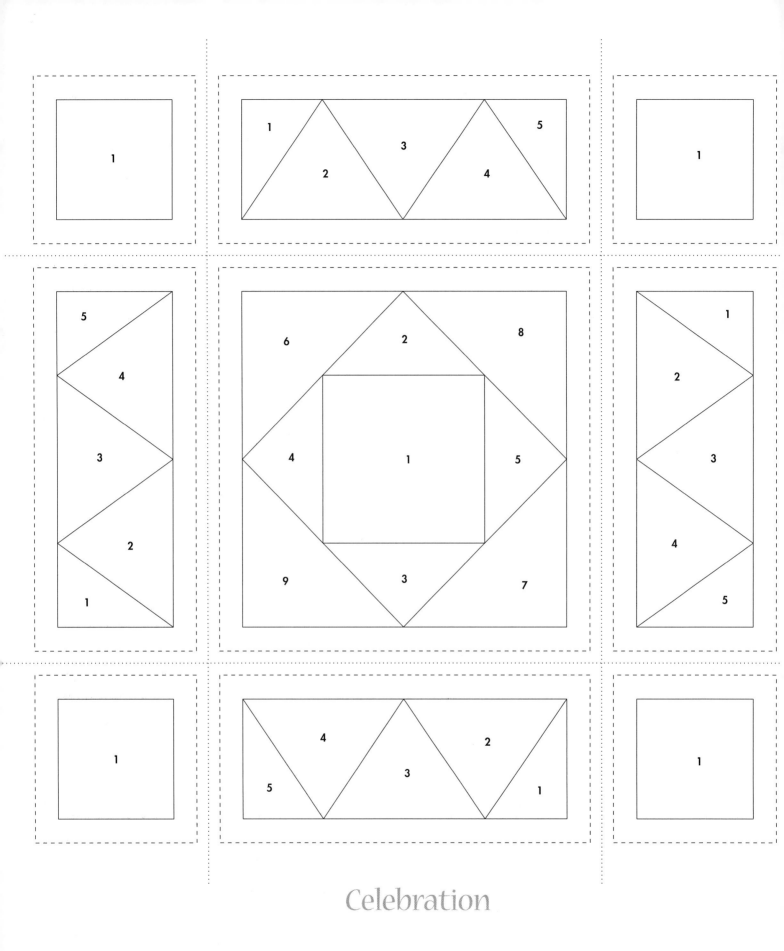

Celebration

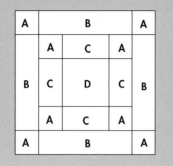

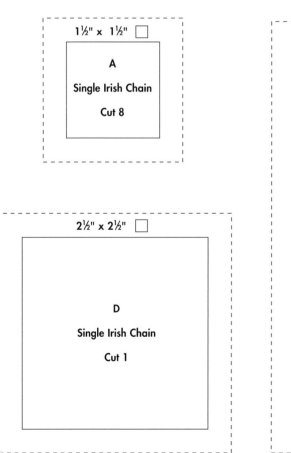

1½" x 1½" ☐

A

Single Irish Chain

Cut 8

2½" x 2½" ☐

D

Single Irish Chain

Cut 1

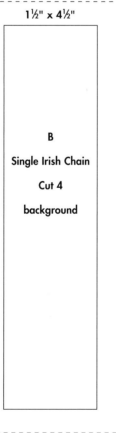

1½" x 4½"

B

Single Irish Chain

Cut 4

background

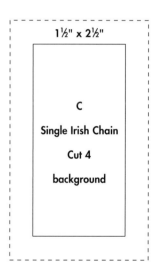

1½" x 2½"

C

Single Irish Chain

Cut 4

background

HELPFUL HINTS

As always, fold the foundation first. There are 6 folds in this foundation. There are 6 pieces to sew to the foundation, but there are eleven pieces that are glued rather than sewn.

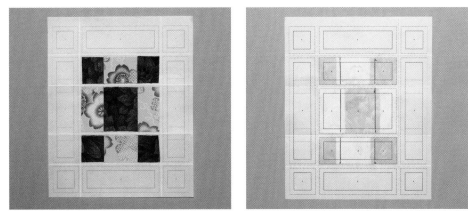

View of front   *View of back*

Piece the center: Sew the nine center pieces of the Single Irish Chain together, press, and lightly glue the edges of the outside pieces to the foundation.

View of front   *View of back*

Join the three center subunits: After refolding, sew both center horizontal seams continuously from side to side, through paper alone, as well as through paper and fabric. In this instance, sew through, rather than skip over the inside seam allowances. Press seams to the side to flatten the block. Clip the four intersections.

View of front   *View of back*

Finishing touches: Glue the remaining eight pieces in place and sew two parallel seams. Do not sew the flaps. Sew continuously through all the seam allowances and fold lines. Press. Clip the four intersections. Sew the remaining two seams. Press and true up.

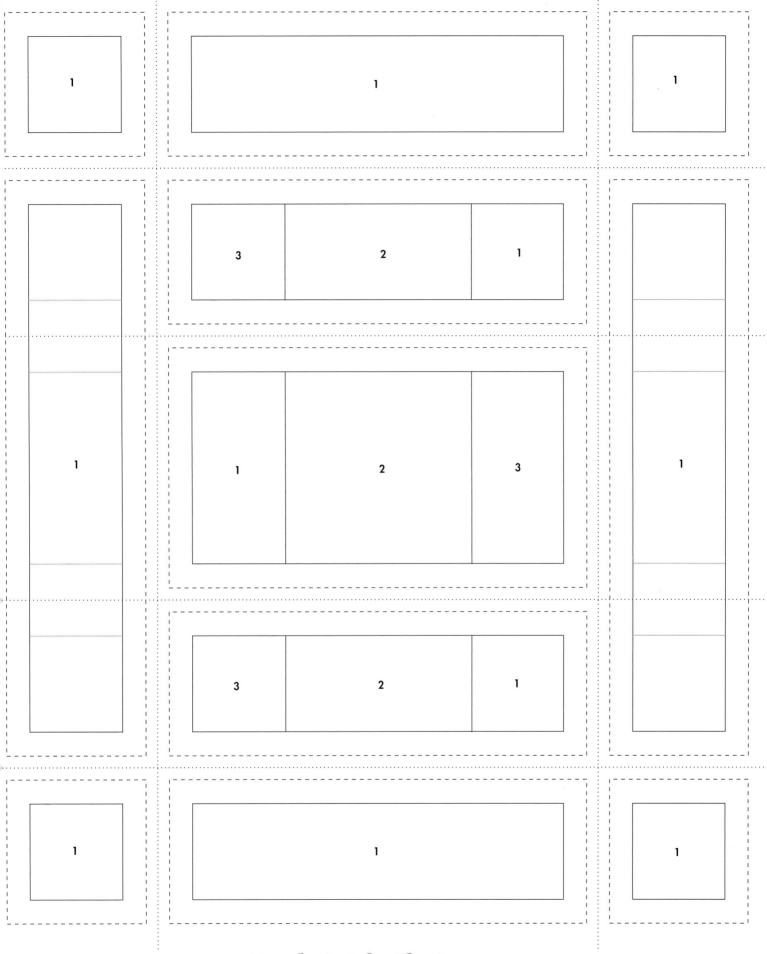

Single Irish Chain 2023

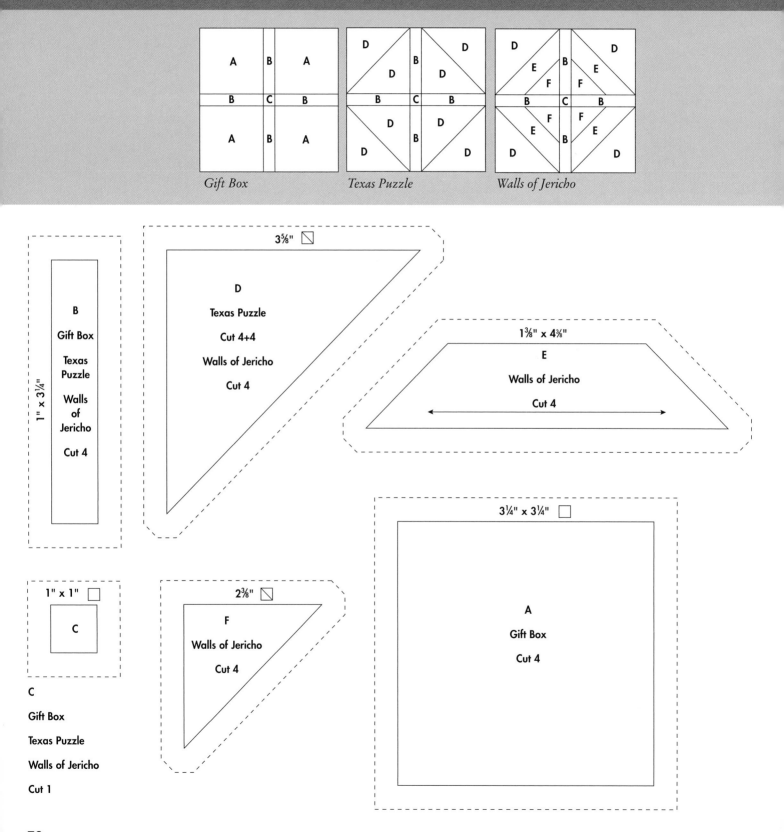

Gift Box *Texas Puzzle* *Walls of Jericho*

B
Gift Box
Texas Puzzle
Walls of Jericho
Cut 4
1" x 3¼"

3⅝"
D
Texas Puzzle
Cut 4+4
Walls of Jericho
Cut 4

1⅜" x 4⅜"
E
Walls of Jericho
Cut 4

1" x 1"
C

C
Gift Box
Texas Puzzle
Walls of Jericho
Cut 1

2⅜"
F
Walls of Jericho
Cut 4

3¼" x 3¼"
A
Gift Box
Cut 4

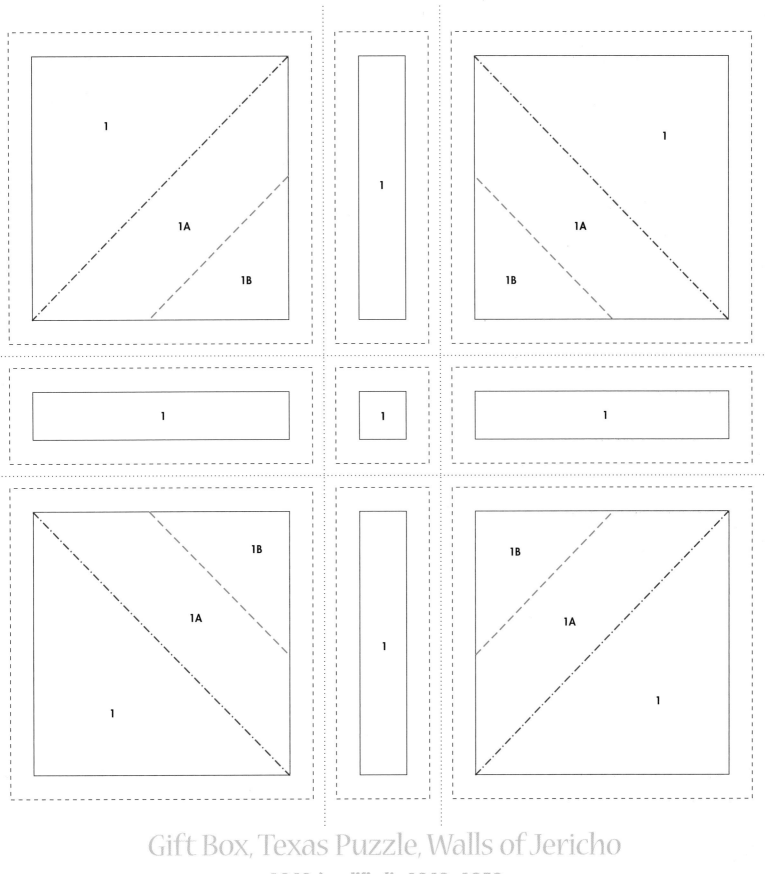

Gift Box, Texas Puzzle, Walls of Jericho

1848 (modified), 1848, 1853

The White Square Quilt, Shoofly Variation, Grandmother's Choice, Crazy Ann, Whirling Five-Patch 1866, 1847, 1855a, 1856, 185[...]

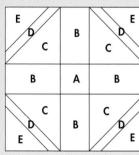 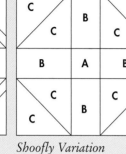 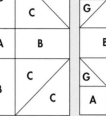 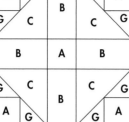 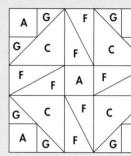 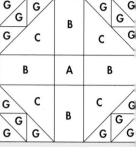 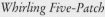

The White Square Quilt *Shoofly Variation* *Grandmother's Choice* *Crazy Ann* *Whirling Five-Patch*

1¾" x 1¾" ☐

A

The White Square Quilt

Shoofly Variation

Whirling Five-Patch

Cut 1

A

Grandmother's Choice

Crazy Ann

Cut 5

1¾" x 2⅞"

B

The White Square Quilt

Shoofly Variation

Grandmother's Choice

Whirling Five-Patch

Cut 4

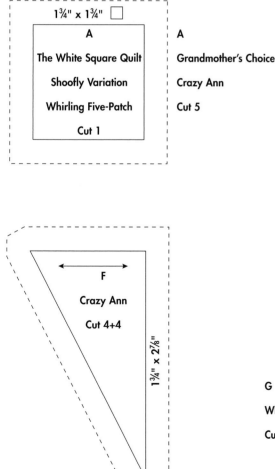

F

Crazy Ann

Cut 4+4

1¾" x 2⅞"

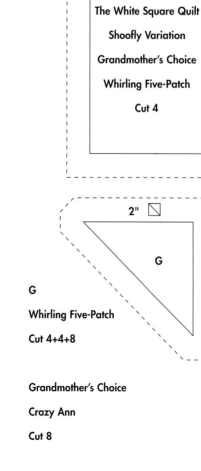

2" ☐

G

G

Whirling Five-Patch

Cut 4+4+8

Grandmother's Choice

Crazy Ann

Cut 8

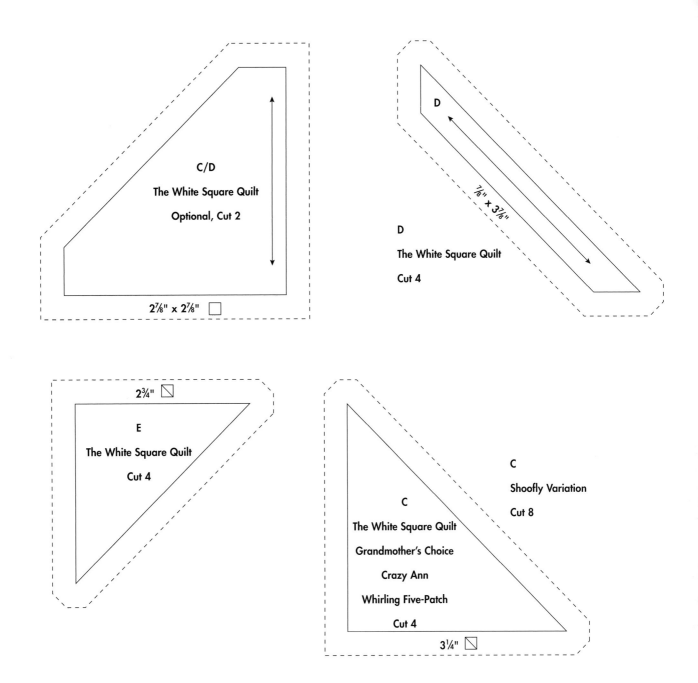

C/D

The White Square Quilt

Optional, Cut 2

2⅞" x 2⅞" ▢

D

⅞" x 3⅞"

D

The White Square Quilt

Cut 4

2¾" ◺

E

The White Square Quilt

Cut 4

C

Shoofly Variation

Cut 8

C

The White Square Quilt

Grandmother's Choice

Crazy Ann

Whirling Five-Patch

Cut 4

3¼" ◺

HELPFUL HINTS

The four corner triangles of The White Square Quilt block are smaller than the four inside triangles. To create the optical illusion in Good and Plenty *(page 76), Michele cut a pair of the inside triangles (template C), which were diagonally opposite of each other, from the same black fabric used for both the rectangles and the skinny diagonal strips. If you deviate from the traditional coloring as she did, save a step and use the optional pattern C/D rather than sewing C to D.*

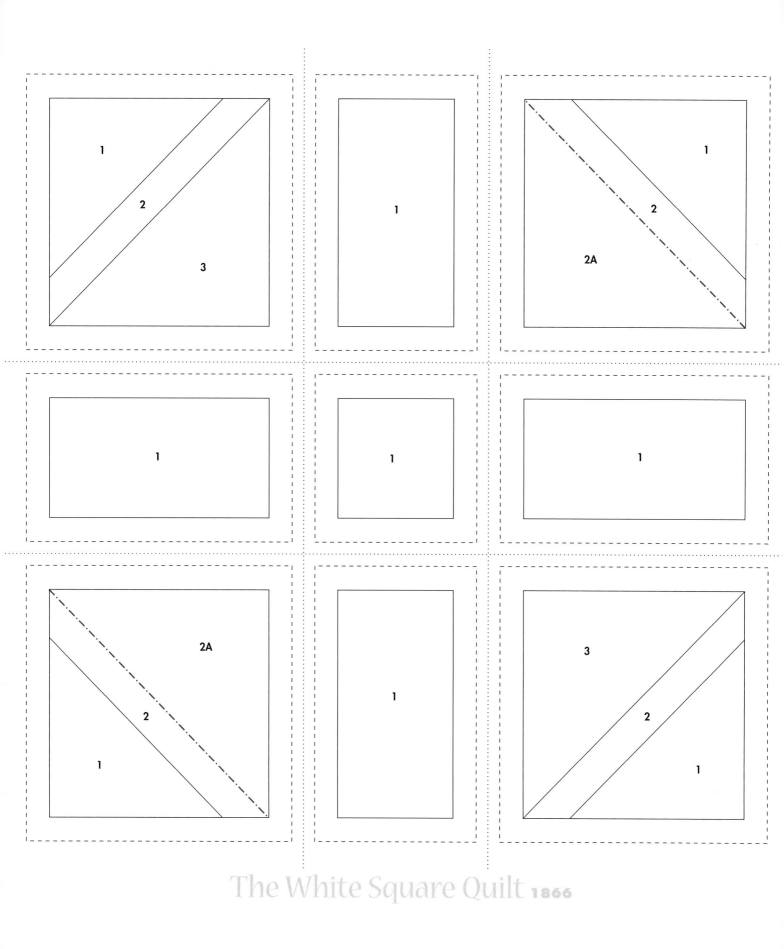

The White Square Quilt 1866

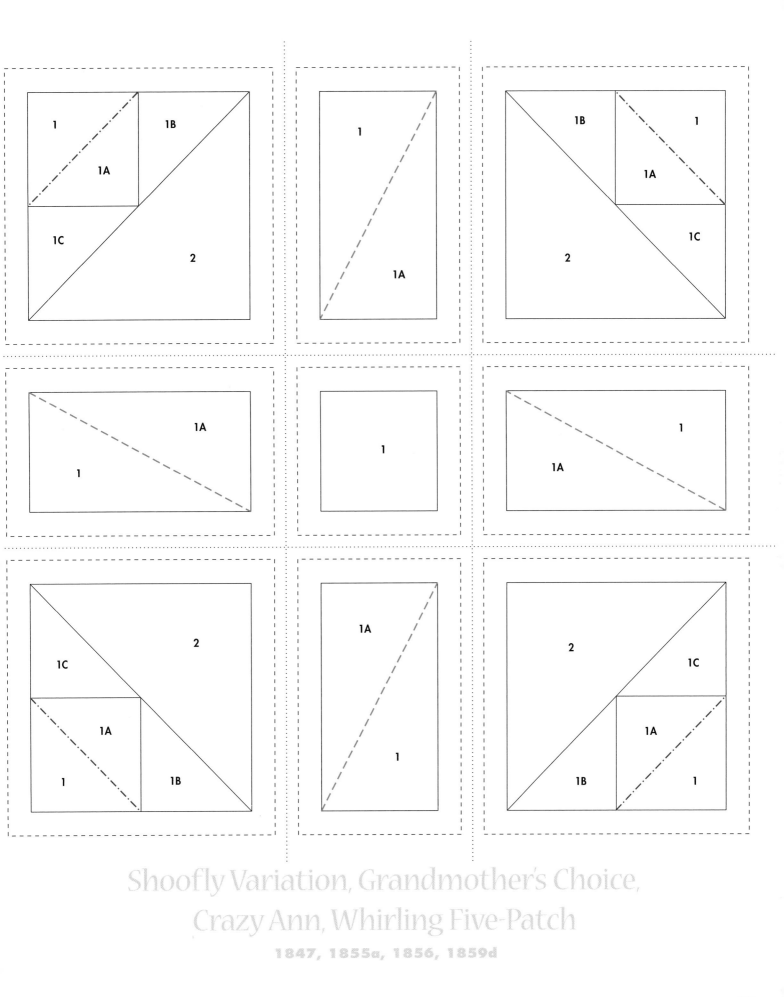

Shoofly Variation, Grandmother's Choice,
Crazy Ann, Whirling Five-Patch
1847, 1855a, 1856, 1859d

Good and Plenty

by Michele Shatz, Delray Beach, FL

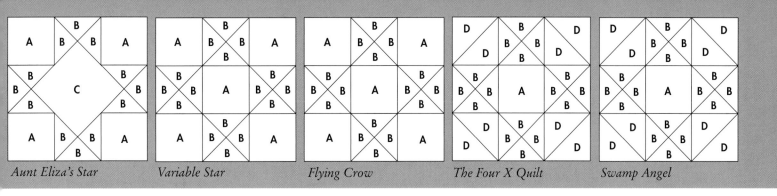

| Aunt Eliza's Star | Variable Star | Flying Crow | The Four X Quilt | Swamp Angel |

HELPFUL HINTS

At first glance, these blocks, pieced by John Willcox, bring quarter-square triangle construction to mind, but that's not how they were made. Traditionally categorized as Nine-Patches, the blocks have been redrafted as Make It Simpler X-9s.

The quickest block to make in this group is Aunt Eliza's Star. Begin by folding the foundation, then cut the fabric and glue the four corner squares in place. Glue a triangle in place on each square and sew. Press the triangles open and lightly glue their tips to the foundation. Position, sew, press, and glue the remaining four adjacent triangles. Glue the large square and the four stand-alone triangles into position. Lastly, sew the subunits together. The corners of the Variable Star are squares as well, but the corners of the other blocks are pieced from triangles. The centers of the other blocks are pieced from a square and four triangles. Since this pattern is 8½" wide, the outside edge of one or two side triangles will not print when it is photocopied. This is not a concern, because the edges of the patterns aren't used as trimming guides.

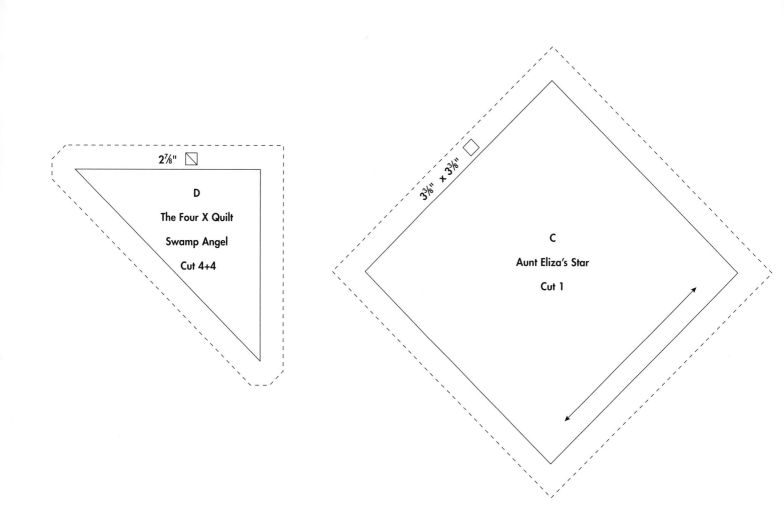

2⅞" ◻

D

The Four X Quilt

Swamp Angel

Cut 4+4

3⅜" x 3⅜" ◻

C

Aunt Eliza's Star

Cut 1

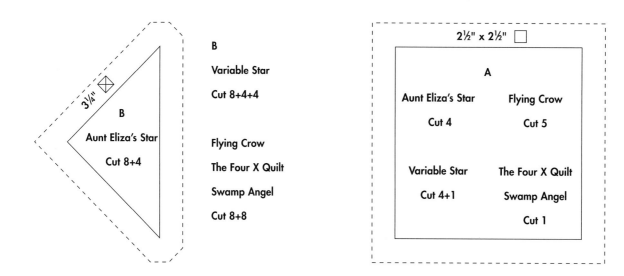

3¼" ◻

B

Aunt Eliza's Star

Cut 8+4

B

Variable Star

Cut 8+4+4

Flying Crow

The Four X Quilt

Swamp Angel

Cut 8+8

2½" x 2½" ◻

A

Aunt Eliza's Star

Cut 4

Flying Crow

Cut 5

Variable Star

Cut 4+1

The Four X Quilt

Swamp Angel

Cut 1

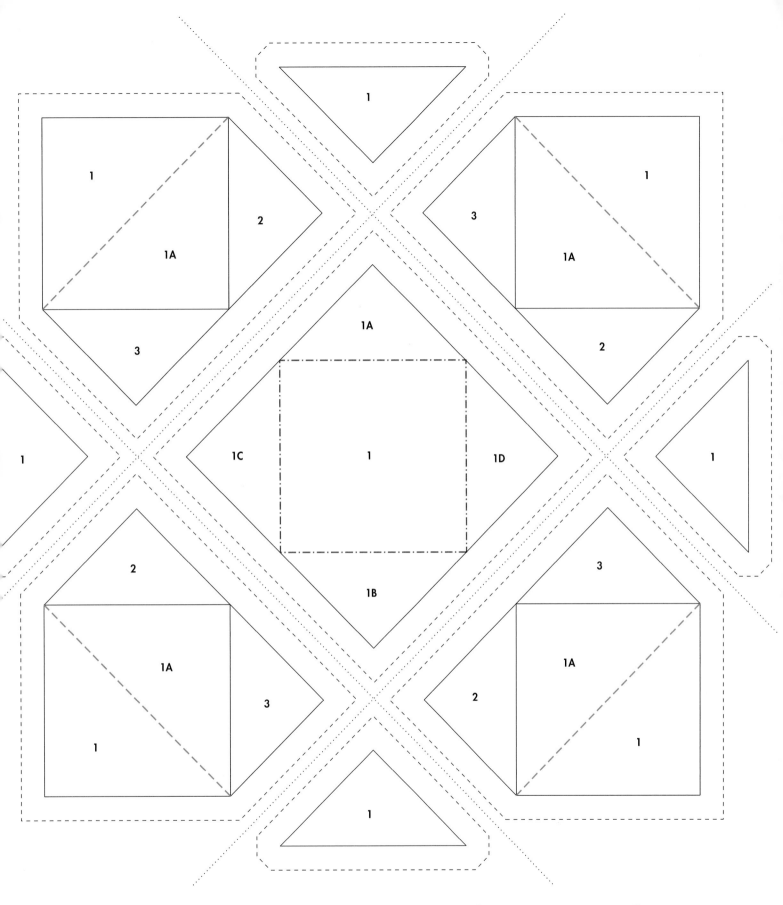

Aunt Eliza's Star, Variable Star, Flying Crow, The Four X Quilt, Swamp Angel 2830, 1631d, 1631e, 1632a, 1632b

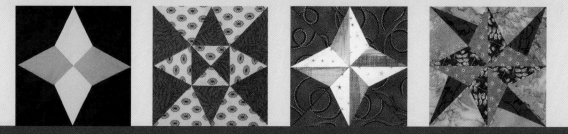

Mill and Stars; Mill and Stars Cornered; Star and Dot; Eight Pointed Star, Askew 2324, 2324 (modified), 1235, 1237a

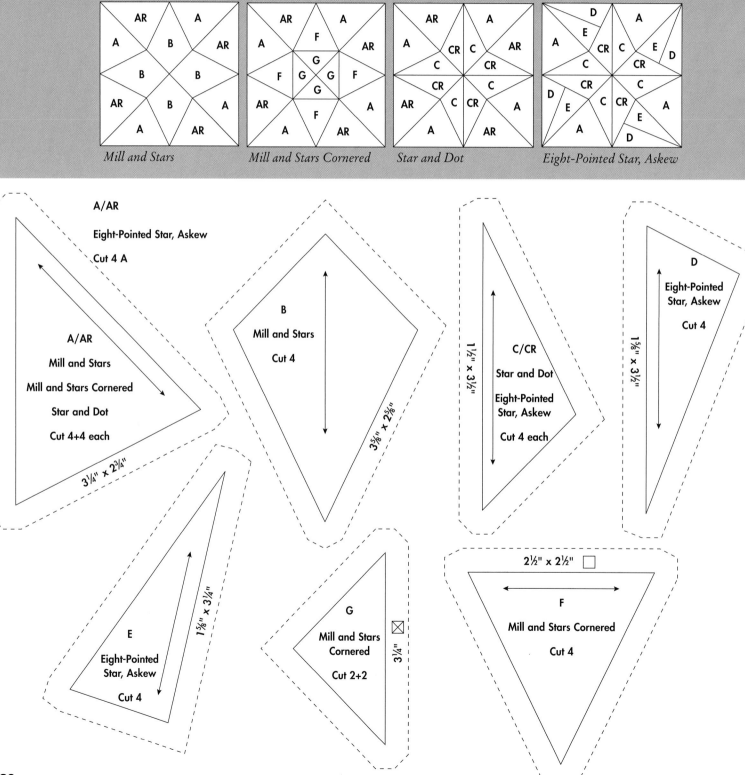

Mill and Stars *Mill and Stars Cornered* *Star and Dot* *Eight-Pointed Star, Askew*

A/AR

Eight-Pointed Star, Askew

Cut 4 A

A/AR
Mill and Stars
Mill and Stars Cornered
Star and Dot
Cut 4+4 each

3¼" x 2¾"

B
Mill and Stars
Cut 4

3⅜" x 2⅝"

C/CR
Star and Dot
Eight-Pointed Star, Askew
Cut 4 each

1½" x 3½"

D
Eight-Pointed Star, Askew
Cut 4

1⅝" x 3½"

E
Eight-Pointed Star, Askew
Cut 4

1⅝" x 3¼"

G
Mill and Stars Cornered
Cut 2+2

3¼"

F
Mill and Stars Cornered
Cut 4

2½" x 2½"

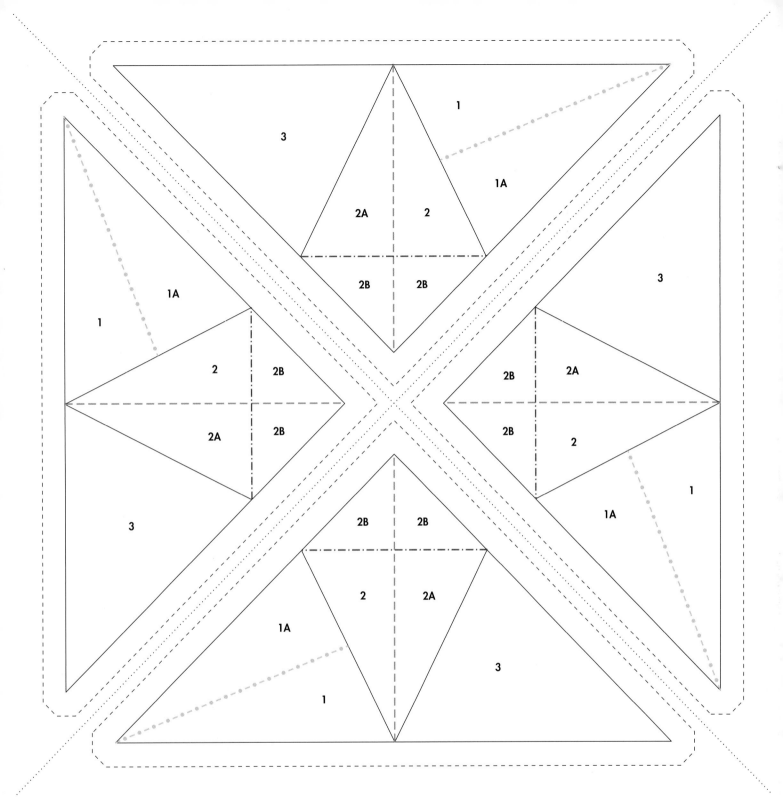

Mill and Stars; Mill and Stars Cornered; Star
and Dot; Eight-Pointed Star, Askew

2324, 2324 (modified), 1235, 1237a

Each of these blocks has at least one template that requires a reverse of itself. To cut reverse patches, place the fabric right side up on the mat. Place the template with the printed side up on the fabric and cut out the piece. For the reverse patch, place the fabric right side up, but turn the template over so the blank side faces up.

Note that on the Star and Dot block, the same fabric is used for both A and AR, but C and CR each require a different fabric.

To avoid a pile of miscut fabric, when making any block for the first time, cut only enough pieces for one block.

You can cut many pieces at once by stacking the fabric right side up and positioning the template either up or down as required to cut out multiple patches.

This shortcut simultaneously makes several pairs of a patch and its reverse: Fold a strip of fabric a few times. Half of the fabric will face up and half will face down. With the template printed side up on the folded strip, cut through all of the layers. Half of the pieces will be right side up, while the others will be wrong side up. Flip the wrong-side-up pieces right sides up and you'll see they are the reverse of the other pieces.

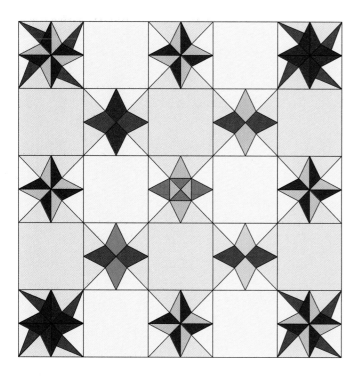

Stellar Assortment

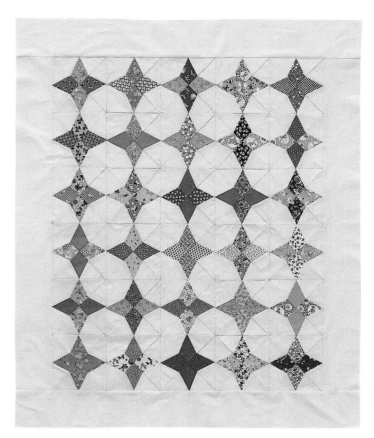

Mill and Stars

by Barbara Shuff Feinstein and
Emily Shuff Klainberg, New York, NY

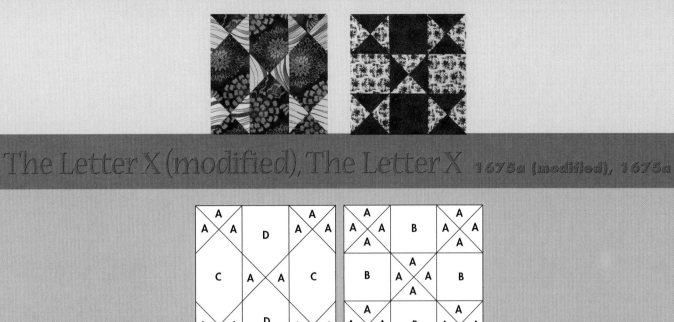

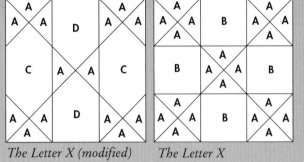

The Letter X (modified)   The Letter X

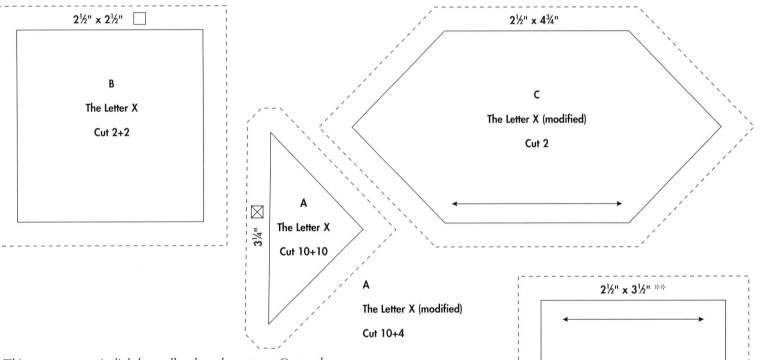

2½" x 2½" ☐

B

The Letter X

Cut 2+2

2½" x 4¾"

C

The Letter X (modified)

Cut 2

⊠   3¼"

A

The Letter X

Cut 10+10

A

The Letter X (modified)

Cut 10+4

2½" x 3½" ✳✳

D

The Letter X (modified)

Cut 2

✳✳ This measurement is slightly smaller than the pattern. Cut to the
size indicated. The tip will be blunted for ease in block construction.

HELPFUL HINTS

I was smitten by an antique quilt made of small pastel triangles on a white background. It was set with airy alternating white blocks. In retrospect, I believe it was a
Letter X quilt. I modified the block by combining squares and triangles into templates C and D to cut down on piecing.

The center square of the original version of The Letter X is made of four triangles.
The character of the block depends on which pair of the four center triangles is
light or dark, which will affect the coloring of the adjoining 2½" squares. It's a great
block to alternate with any in the Aunt Eliza's Star group (pages 77–79).

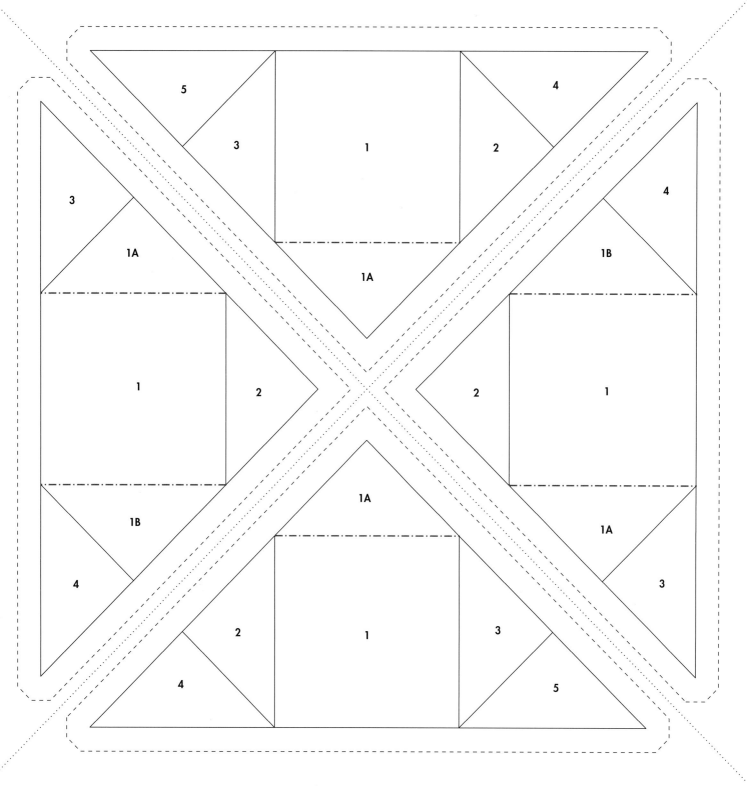

The Letter X (modified), The Letter X

1675a (modified), 1675a

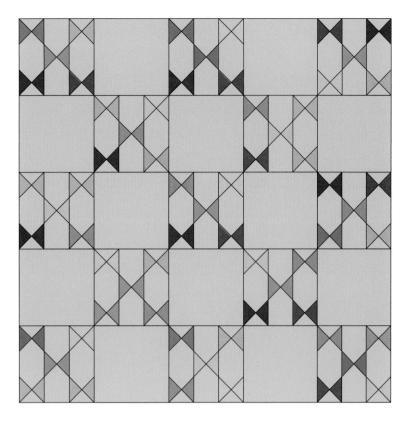

The Letter X (modified)

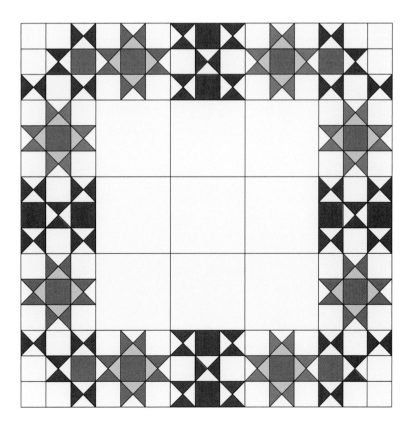

The Letter X
with unpieced corners, set with the Variable Star block
(page 77)

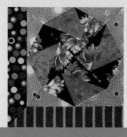

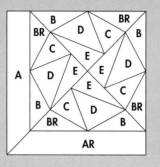

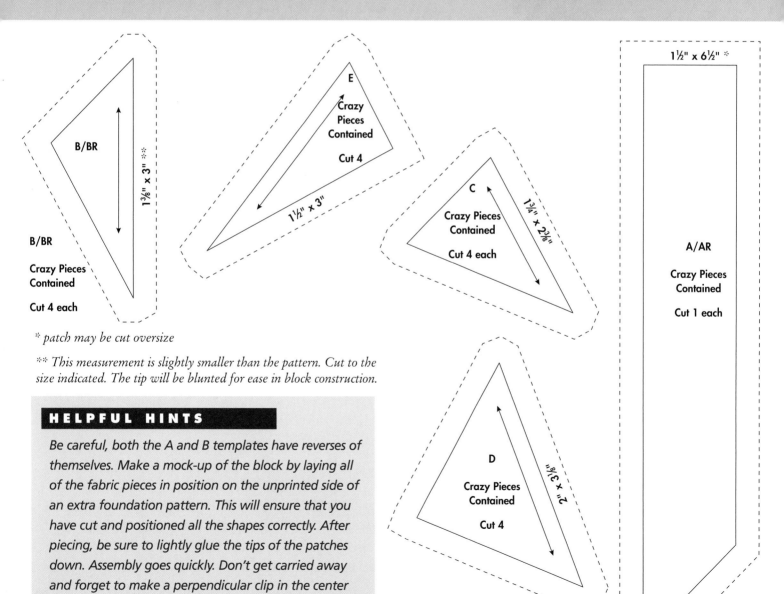

B/BR

$1\frac{3}{8}" \times 3"$ **

B/BR

Crazy Pieces
Contained

Cut 4 each

E

Crazy
Pieces
Contained

Cut 4

$1\frac{1}{2}" \times 3"$

C

Crazy Pieces
Contained

Cut 4 each

$1\frac{3}{4}" \times 2\frac{3}{8}"$

$1\frac{1}{2}" \times 6\frac{1}{2}"$ *

A/AR

Crazy Pieces
Contained

Cut 1 each

D

Crazy Pieces
Contained

Cut 4

$2" \times 3\frac{3}{8}"$

* *patch may be cut oversize*

** *This measurement is slightly smaller than the pattern. Cut to the
size indicated. The tip will be blunted for ease in block construction.*

HELPFUL HINTS

*Be careful, both the A and B templates have reverses of
themselves. Make a mock-up of the block by laying all
of the fabric pieces in position on the unprinted side of
an extra foundation pattern. This will ensure that you
have cut and positioned all the shapes correctly. After
piecing, be sure to lightly glue the tips of the patches
down. Assembly goes quickly. Don't get carried away
and forget to make a perpendicular clip in the center
intersection before sewing the second diagonal seam.*

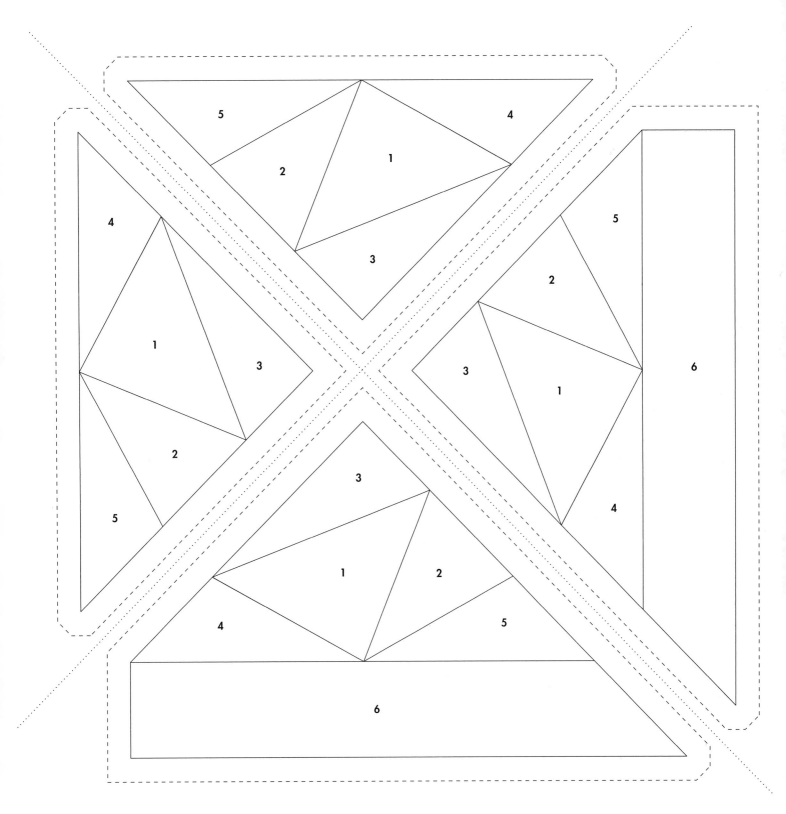

Crazy Pieces Contained 2354 (modified)

Gizmos

by Susan Stauber, New York, NY

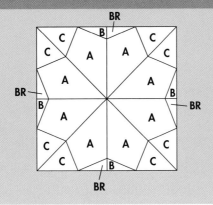

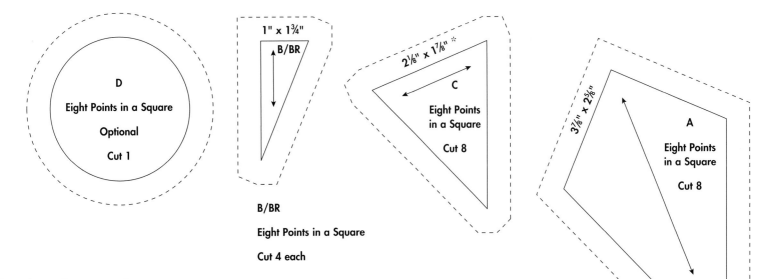

D

Eight Points in a Square

Optional

Cut 1

1" x 1¾"

B/BR

B/BR

Eight Points in a Square

Cut 4 each

2⅛" x 1⅞" ✳

C

Eight Points
in a Square

Cut 8

3⅞" x 2⅝"

A

Eight Points
in a Square

Cut 8

✳ *patch may be cut oversize*

HELPFUL HINTS

Sew the vertical seam from the edge to the center of the block. Stop sewing one stitch before the seam allowance. Shorter stitches may give you more control. Backstitch and lift your needle. Don't sew through any seam allowances. Resume sewing the remaining vertical seam to the edge of the block. Clip the intersection. Sew the horizontal seam in the same manner. Never sew through an interior seam allowance or through any flaps.

Both diagonal seams are sewn the same way. Begin at the edge of the block or in the center. As you reach the block's center, trim away any excess paper in the center if it's in your way. Don't trim any paper that has lines printed on it. Clip the intersection. Sew the next diagonal seam. Clip the intersection. Press the seams in a clockwise direction.

To make a Dresden Plate-like block, appliqué shape D (seam allowance included) over the center of each block once the top has been assembled and the foundation paper subsequently removed.

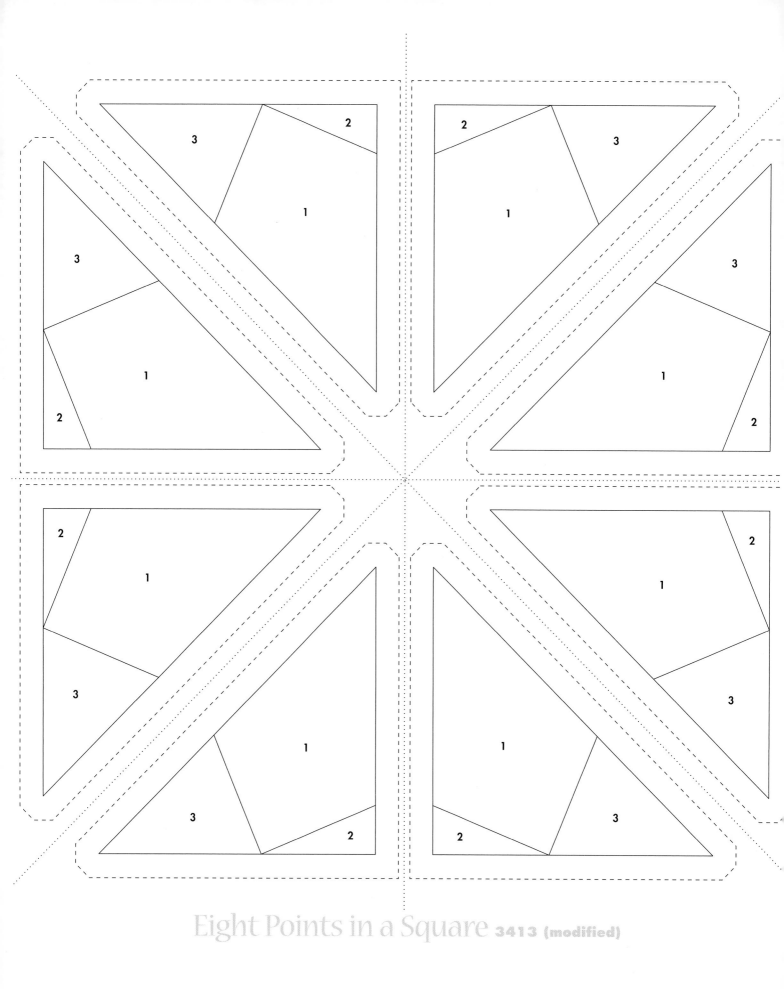

Eight Points in a Square 3413 (modified)

Quarter-Square Triangle Block 2301

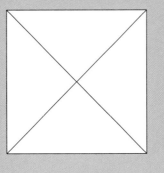

This Quarter-Square Triangle block pattern can be used to make any size block, 6" finished or smaller. It's an easy way to sew four triangles together with a perfect Make It Simpler center.

1. Choose 2, 3, or 4 different fabrics. Refer to the chart and cut one square from each fabric. Cut the squares of fabric in half diagonally, twice. There will be leftover pieces if you make only one block.

2. Place the pieces and sew the foundation together in the Make It Simpler manner (pages 8–18).

3. Fold the block in half diagonally (corner to corner). Using a square rotary cutting ruler larger than the desired unfinished size of the block, align the diagonal of the ruler on the center seam. Refer to page 40 and trim around the template, lining up the ruler's diagonal. True up the folded block to the desired unfinished size, using the measurements on the rotary cutting ruler.

Finished Block Size	Unfinished Block Size (true-up size)	Size to Cut Squares
1"	1½"	2¼"
2"	2½"	3¼"
3"	3½"	4¼"
4"	4½"	5¼"
4¼"	4¾"	5½"
4½"	5"	5¾"
4¾"	5¼"	6"
5"	5½"	6¼"
5¼"	5¾"	6½"
5½"	6"	6¾"
5¾"	6¼"	7"
6"	6½"	7¼"

Quarter-Square Triangle Block 2301

Constance Benson and Denise Bradley
QUILTING . . . that's what friends are for.

Pamela Creason, Christine Taylor, and Andrea Verzantvoort
Friends extraordinaire.

Barbara Shuff Feinstein and Emily Shuff Klainberg
Identical twins, but not identical quilts.

Carol Goossens'
Daughter of an excellent quilter.

Dorothea Hahn
Reluctant piecer; appliqué enthusiast.

Addy Harkavy
Queen of the fabric stash and
leader of the (dog) pack.

Sylvia Hughes
Fabricaholic, opera-loving jazz fan.

Linda Kraynack
Passionate quilter, wife, and mother.

Marcella Peek
Quilter without a stash.

Janice E. Petre
Longarm machine quilter, wife, Mom, Nana,
Red Hat Diva, fabricaholic.

Ellen Quinn
Following Aunt Mary in quilting.

Jeri Riggs
Ex-psychiatrist turned fanatical quilter.

Michele Shatz
Born quilter.

Susan Stauber
Have paper, will piece.

Robin Strauss
Brooklyn quilter who loves Bronx Bombers. "Go Yankees!"

The Riverbank Quilters
Lynette V. Baker, Constance Benson, Ivy Bonsu-Anane, Denise Bradley, Ms. Hetty Doldron, Frances Jackson, Alice Liverman, Ethel McCall, Louise G. McCrae, Adelaide M. Walker, and Barbara J. Wane at Riverbank State Park (New York, NY)
A work in progress.

John Willcox
The running quilter.

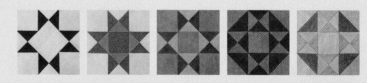

Adrienne Yorinks
Textile artist, poodle lover, and newlywed.

Ask for a free catalog:

C&T Publishing, Inc.

P.O. Box 1456

Lafayette, CA 94549

800-284-1114

email: ctinfo@ctpub.com

website: www.ctpub.com

Cotton Patch Mail Order

3404 Hall Lane

Dept CTB

Lafayette, CA 94549

800-835-4418   925-283-7883

email: quiltusa@yahoo.com

website: www.quiltusa.com

Note: Fabrics used in the quilts shown may not be currently available because fabric manufacturers keep most fabrics in print for only a short time.

ABOUT THE AUTHOR

Anita Grossman Solomon is an award-winning quilter and quilting instructor who invented "Make It Simpler" techniques to make quilting faster and easier. She has a degree in art and brings a fresh perspective to the quiltmaking process. Anita lives in New York City. She can be contacted at www.makeitsimpler.com.

**Another book by
Anita Grossman Solomon**

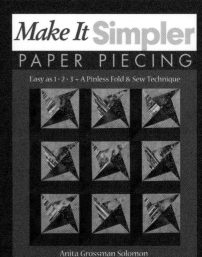